OHANA

LOVE, GRIEF, AND HOPE IN THE TIME OF THE OPIOID CRISIS

Sonderho Press, Prescott K0E 1T0

Published by Sonderho Press.

Printed in Canada.

ISBN: 978-1-7386952-8-7

This book is printed on acid-free paper.

Cover artwork, "Surfer Silhouette II", painted by and used with the permission
of artist John Collins.

Photograph of Roger Wong taken by Jordan Anderson, used with permission.

Back cover photograph of Mauna Lani Beach was taken, and gifted to the
author, by a friend.

OHANA

LOVE, GRIEF, AND HOPE IN THE TIME OF THE OPIOID CRISIS

A MEMOIR BY IRENE REILLY

SONDERHO PRESS

"In this remarkable book, Irene Reilly walks us through her journey of love, loss, and grief. She puts her vulnerability as a mother on the page and shows us that human resiliency can push darkness away so that hope can grow. Heartfelt and honest, I highly recommend it."

— *Marina Nemat, author,* Prisoner of Tehran *and* After Tehran

---

"In this memoir about the loss of her son, Roger, to a fentanyl poisoning, Irene Reilly courageously bares her soul. We join her in her journey from first learning of Roger's death to enduring all the firsts of the following year without his presence. This is an important book for anyone experiencing this trauma, as well as those trying to support them. Love and resilience spring from every page as Irene's Ohana provides her with the strength she needs, and her advocacy work provides her with purpose. There is something remarkable about mothers who have lost a child who raise awareness and advocate so others will not face the same tragedy."

— *Angie Hamilton, Executive Director,*
  Families for Addiction Recovery

"Reading *Ohana: Love, Grief, and Hope in the Time of the Opioid Crisis* brought me right back to the raw reality of working in addiction recovery—the pain, the losses, the small victories that feel like mountains, and the heartbreaking truth that this disease never affects just one person; it's a family disease. Roger wasn't just a client; he left a mark on all of us—a hole in our hearts that will never truly heal. But what stayed with me most was Irene. Somehow, through all her pain, she found a way to give love back tenfold. She treated every person in our care like they were her own son. This book is not just about grief—it's about resilience, love, and the incredible capacity of the human spirit to give even when it's broken. Roger will never be forgotten."

— *Jordan Anderson, Executive Director of Alpha House*

"In this heart-rending firsthand account of her son Roger's lost struggle with recovery from opioid addiction, Irene Reilly writes, 'everyone is somebody's someone'. This is a timely, haunting, and ultimately inspiring glimpse into Irene's courageous recovery from shattered to whole, and of the many other lives connected to her loss. As Irene's heart unclenches, light slowly overcomes once-crippling darkness. This is an intimate, raw, and powerful memoir."

— *Siobhan Lant, Director of Volunteers and Programs,*
   Writers Collective of Canada

"Irene's inspirational story reminds us that even in tragedy there is hope. While the overdose toll is often presented as just numbers, Irene shines a light into its darkest corners, offering unique insights earned from the tragedy of losing her son Roger, 'somebody's someone', to overdose. Irene is unique and also one of the many who drive International Overdose Awareness Day in their local communities, helping others heal from loss and generously trying to end overdose for those of us with a living chance. We should care like we are all family; in Ohana, Irene shows us how."

— *John Ryan, CEO, International Overdose Awareness Day*

"Having one's child die is an indescribable pain. Knowing that death was preventable and witnessing thousands more join the ranks of the grieving makes it more excruciating. In Ohana, Irene takes us on this journey, showing us the pain and the hope as she honours Roger's legacy, connects with others who knew and loved him, and engages in advocacy to bring attention to the opioid crisis. Anyone who has experienced pain or loss, anyone who is a friend or ally, will find solace and fullness of heart by reading *Ohana: Love, Grief, and Hope in the Time of the Opioid Crisis.*"

— *Petra Shultz, Co-founder, Moms Stop the Harm*

Dedication

In loving memory of Roger
You live on in my heart and in the hearts of all who knew you.

To my precious son Brandon
You grew up with grace in the shadow of Roger's illness.

To my Ohana

Jenifer, Lucy, Jill, Lee, Lorraine, and Lesley and all my friends.
I would not be standing today without you

Landy Anderson and Family
You opened your hearts to Roger and extended your love to me.

And to Henry, Roger and Brandon's dad, our family began, in love, with us.

Each of you is woven into my heart
and into the pages of this book.

Ohana is the Hawaiian word for family; its meaning is both simple and complex. Ohana includes the people to whom you're related, as well as the larger group of folks outside your bloodline who support and sustain you, to whom you feel indebted and responsible.

Roger was raised on the Big Island of Hawaii from the time he was a baby to twenty years of age. He was truly a local boy, and the island culture shaped his sensitive nature and Aloha spirit.

Author's Note

This book contains subject matter regarding grief, mental health, and addiction that may be disturbing or upsetting. Please take care.

For support in Ontario, contact:

ConnexOntario | Mental Health & Addiction Treatment Services

www.connexontario.ca
1-866-531-2600

Elsewhere, please seek resources in your local province or country.

Contents

Woven 1

The End of My World 3

Coming Together 9

Arrivals 16

Carpet Diem 28

How Fragile We Are 31

No One Ever is to Blame 34

My Return to Life 39

Roger Memorial Art Contest 44

Recovery Day 48

The Salmon Run 51

A Pain With a Name 53

Let Go and Let God 56

Do Something Prime Minister 58

Calling All Angels 65

We Grieve Thousands 73

The Assembly Line 78

A Tale of Two Tables 82

People Die All the Time 87

Who Will Fix Me Now? 92

My Road to Recovery 95

Flags of Hope Toronto 98

Climbing the Wall 105

Surfer Silhouette 110

About the Author 116

Acknowledgements 117

Resources 119

Woven

by Becky Hemsley
2023

You're sewn into my habits,
Like the way I make my tea,
You're stitched within my waking hours,
Threaded through my dreams
The fibres of you run through
Words and phrases that I say
And all my memories of you
Embroider every day
The jokes you told embellish days
That otherwise are bare
And all your little quirks make up
My life of patchwork squares
It's you that knitted colour,
That tied knots and bonds so strong
That your beauty and your essence
Still remain now you are gone
See, we are like a tapestry
All stitched and woven tight
And I know you're always with me
In the fabric of my life
So when I start to feel things
Tangled up inside my heart
I stop and realise love
Is an enduring work of art

The End of My World

Scene 1 – The Police Station
Thursday, June 15, 2017, 3 p.m.

The afternoon sun scorched the glass and white-concrete facade of the 52nd Division Police Station as we waded across the broad forecourt to the entrance. Traffic screeched past us towards Chinatown. Pedestrians battled the congestion. Sweat dripped down my back, my nerves frayed with dread. We pushed through the heavy doors. A blast of air conditioning enveloped us as we proceeded towards the counter where a uniformed officer sat cocooned in a glass cell. He was a big, burly man with a no-nonsense expression on his face.

"How can I help you?" he bellowed.

Shrunken by the counter's height, I tiptoed to project my voice through the perforated partition.

"I'm here to file a missing person's report," I said in a shaky voice.

"What makes you suspect a missing person?"

"It's my son. He hasn't answered his phone or text. I'm worried."

"Name, date of birth?" the officer shook his head as if to say, *"Ma'am, if we investigated everyone who doesn't answer their phone …"*

"Roger Wong, born 31 October 1988. He's in recovery. He didn't return to his group home last night. I don't know where he is."

The officer avoided eye contact as he bent over his computer screen, tapping away at the keys.

"Is he native?" he asked.

"He often gets cast as Indigenous looking," I answered. "He's half Chinese with long black hair. Have you found him?"

"Please take a seat," he motioned to a row of chairs lining the white wall. "I'm checking."

I held my breath as we sat down.

"He's checking. That's good, isn't it?" I said to Roger's friend Evonne, who had accompanied me.

"See, he's printing paperwork. He's found him." I clung to hope.

"It's not good. Prepare yourself," she said.

In my mind, the worst-case scenario was that Roger had relapsed. Maybe the police had picked him up. My thoughts spun back to previous relapses. We'd always found him, eventually.

It's not the end of the world, I thought. My brain was already calling the detox centre. We can do this.

The officer walked towards the back of the office, papers in hand.

I inhaled, but the air struggled to pass the lump in my throat as a whimper escaped.

"They've found Roger. Look at all those papers. They've got him."

My words floated to the high ceiling.

Finally, a plain-clothed officer strode out from behind the counter.

"Follow me, please," he said. One of his hands held the stack of papers, the other the door.

He took us into a windowless, monochromatic interview room. A round table flanked by four swivelling office chairs awaited us. It appeared dark compared to the bright foyer we had just been in.

"Take a seat," he gestured towards the table.

"Have you found him? Have you found my son?"

"There's no easy way to tell you this. Your son is dead," he said as he dropped the papers on the table.

My heart heaved. His words ricocheted around the room. I wanted to push them back into his mouth, stop them from entering my ears.

"No, no, God no ... No, you've got it wrong." I tried to focus, but the room spun, the walls closed in. A guttural cry tore from some prehistoric chamber in my heart. "Noooooo ...!"

"Can I get you water? Is there someone you'd like to call?" he asked. He may have said more before leaving the room. Everything went black.

I crumpled to the floor, nauseated. My body refused to absorb the news that Roger was dead. Evonne sat in silent shock. We were drowning in the same whirlpool, but I couldn't reach out to help her. I couldn't help myself. I groped my way back onto the chair.

Is there someone you'd like to call? The officer's words seeped through the haze. I called Caro, who worked nearby and had worried with me over the past two days as our texts to Roger went unanswered.

"Caro, it's Irene. I'm at the 52nd Division. They've found Roger. He died."

Caro was a close friend from Roger's time in recovery at the Renascent Rehab program. She had interviewed Roger and me in 2014, documenting his journey through addiction and recovery. The *Renascent Alumni Report* featured his story. Roger had touched so many hearts in the program. Back then, his recovery had given hope to others.

The next thing I recall was the officer back in the room and Caro with her laptop open, asking questions, taking notes. I heard fragments of sentences: "... suspected drug overdose ... police report ... the body at the coroner's ... call to make arrangements...."

The scene froze. I froze. Unable to rewind or press play, I floated outside my body as if in a dream, a nightmare.

The officer said something about his daughter's graduation. He had to leave and handed me his card. On the back, he wrote the coroner's phone number.

We staggered out of the room, then out of the station. The sun blinded us as we sat down on a concrete bench facing Dundas Street West. The same street we had left an hour earlier. But everything had changed.

The police officer's card with the coroner's number was in my hand. The echo of his voice pounded in my head: *"Make arrangements for the body."*

Scene 2 – Alpha House
5 p.m.

It was late afternoon when we arrived at Alpha House, the recovery home where Roger had lived for five months after his relapse and rehab the previous December. Although he had already graduated from the program, this had been his happy place. Roger's friends and counsellors were waiting for us. We congregated in the front living room in a collective anguish, holding each other, crying. I remembered Roger's own grief when his dear friend Hillary passed away only a few months earlier. My heart broke to see him suffering. I felt the vulnerability in the room—young men in recovery who had witnessed too much grief already.

Jordan, the director of Alpha House, ushered me into the office. Caro was by my side as I called Roger's dad in Hawaii. It took every fibre of my strength to dial the familiar 808 area code. Dread and adrenalin coursed through my veins with every ring that echoed across the line. Finally, we connected.

"Henry, is that you?" My tongue could barely move inside my parched mouth.

"Who do you think it is? You dialled my number. What's that noise in the background? Where are you?" he said.

"I'm …"

"Speak up. This is a terrible line."

"I have to … to … tell you."

"Are the boys alright?"

"It's Roger."

"What about Roger?"

I could feel his frustration.

"What's going on with that boy? He never returns my calls. What now?"

"It's Roger … he's gone."

"This bloody line … I can't hear you! I'll call you back."

"No, no please don't hang up, please Henry."

"You're not making any sense, Irene. What the hell is going on?"

I looked at the phone, choking on my words, and I started to sob.

"Irene, what's happening? Are you crying? Stop crying!"

I couldn't speak.

Caro took the phone.

"Henry, are you sitting down? Is anyone with you?" I heard her ask.

Dear Henry, it had been a rough ten years since I left Hawaii and returned to Toronto with the hope of a new start for Roger and his brother Brandon. It was 2007 and Roger had dropped out of high school on the Big Island. The early signs were there, but of what I didn't know until 2010, when Roger joined me and Brandon in Toronto. It was then that I slowly uncovered his addiction to OxyContin and the cycle of relapse and recovery began.

I felt out of my body again. What if I hadn't left? What if I'd known sooner? What if…? This wasn't how it was supposed to end.

I found myself back in the living room, consoling and being consoled by Roger's recovery Ohana. Alpha House was a safe place to absorb the immediate reality of Roger's death.

Scene 3 – Nothing Gold Can Stay
7 p.m.

Lucy, my dear friend who had been in my life since Roger's inception, came to take me home. We had worked together at The Other Café on Bloor Street West, my first job in Toronto after I married Henry on May 1, 1984. One cold February night in 1988, while waitressing at the restaurant, cold sweats and nausea overcame me. I ran to the washroom and looked at my pale face in the mirror. I gagged.

Could it be the flu? I thought. The next day, a doctor confirmed that I was pregnant and told me this "flu" would last eighteen years. Lucy became Aunty Lucy and Roger's godmother. That was twenty-nine years ago. This night, she was by my side consoling me as I shivered, cold and nauseated, one more time.

When we reached the door to my apartment, I saw a business card taped to it. While I was at the police station filing the missing persons report, a police sergeant had been to my door and left his card. On the back he had written, "Irene, please call this number."

What if I had answered the door by myself or come home alone to that note? By the grace of God, Lucy was with me. She helped me inside and poured me a glass of wine. There was one more call I had to make before I fell completely apart. I had to tell my younger son, Brandon, who was visiting our family in Glasgow.

It was after midnight in Scotland. My niece Irene answered the phone.

"Hi, Aunty Irene," she said,

"Irene, is Brandon there?"

"He's sleeping. Are you okay?"

"Roger is gone. He relapsed." The words fell out of my mouth, but I closed my ears to them.

"Oh, my God!" she gasped.

"Don't wake Brandon up now. Let him sleep until morning, then call me."

"I'll get my dad over. Don't worry. We'll make sure he's not alone. We're all here."

Lucy stayed with me through the night. Tomorrow would come too soon.

Coming Together

Friday, June 16, 2017

In the morning, I opened my eyes, and for a moment, I smiled. Sunlight poured through the Venetian blinds, casting slats of light across the familiar cocoon of my bedroom. Then the flood swept over me. Was it a dream, a nightmare? I grabbed the sheets and closed my eyes. In the past, I could jump into action, ready in full armour to fight the dragon of addiction. I had detox centres, rehab facilities, counsellors, and friends all on speed dial. Those numbers were no use to me today.

"Irene, are you awake?" Lucy's sweet voice floated in from the kitchen.

"Would you like a cup of tea?"

"Yes, please."

I never wanted to wake up again. How could the sunrise and the birds sing, pantomiming a glorious summer day? Did they not know my boy was dead? When he was a baby, I sang to him:

> You are my sunshine, my only sunshine,
>
> You make me happy when skies are grey,
>
> You'll never know, dear, how much I love you.
>
> Please, don't take my sunshine away.

The sun dared to shine, but no light entered my heart. I slid my feet onto the floor, testing my legs to see if they would hold my weight. A chill came over me as I recalled the scene at the police station the day before. The police officer's cold words as he handed me the card with the coroner's number.

"Make arrangements for the body."

How could Roger's twenty-eight years of love, laughter, and life be reduced to a body? I trembled. Lucy's voice came to me again.

Lucy stayed until Jill arrived—a tag-team of friendship. Jill, my dear friend of over thirty years, brought me a red Healing Heart teddy bear with a wee tartan heart sewn on its fluffy chest. That bear was stuffed with love. I held it close.

I sat on my warm patio overlooking the Humber ravine. The trees were covered in a flush of golden green, and I thought of Robert Frost's poem, "Nothing Gold Can Stay".

> Nature's first green is gold,
>
> Her hardest hue to hold.
>
> Her early leaf's a flower;
>
> But only so an hour.
>
> Then leaf subsides to leaf.
>
> So Eden sank to grief.
>
> So dawn goes down to day.
>
> Nothing gold can stay.

I dialled the coroner's number. A soft voice answered, "Leave your name and number, and I will return your call within twenty-four hours."

I felt relieved, not knowing if I could have this conversation yet, or ever. Hearing the details would only be confirmation. The sweet tea steamed, and I held the cup to my mouth. I sipped and breathed, gathering the strength to call my Brandon.

On the phone to him, I spoke the unimaginable words: "I'm so sorry Brandon, Roger is gone … a suspected drug overdose. We'll have more details soon. Come home, son."

"Aww Mum …"

It was a brief call. The silence spoke volumes. My heart continued to shatter as I took on the collateral pain.

My family stayed by Brandon's side as they booked his flight from Glasgow to Toronto. A bottle of whiskey was opened as they huddled together in grief.

I had lived in fear of this day for years, throughout Roger's bouts of illness in active opioid addiction. But now my guard was down. He had been six months into recovery and attended his twelve-step program. He was tan and healthy from his work in landscaping and had gained weight. The sparkle was back in his eyes.

Only days before he passed, we had met for dinner at Sushi Maido. His best friends, Justin and Caro, joined us. We had chosen a comfy booth in the back, feasting on plates of sushi rolls and sashimi. The boys had appetites. They laughed as they chatted about Roger's favourite movie with Keanu Reeves as John Wick. He had often been told he looked like Keanu, with his Chinese features and long hair. He liked that. Watching the time, I reminded Roger that we needed to hurry to make his twelve-step meeting at the Hill.

"Mum, we're having a good time, and anyway, we're late. I'll go on the weekend."

It was true, we were having a good time together, and I didn't want to sound like a nag. We enjoyed our meal, not knowing it would be our last supper together. When we left the restaurant, I watched Roger and Justin walk along Bloor Street West towards Spadina Avenue. Roger smiled and waved goodbye.

"I love you," I said.

The coroner returned my call. He took his time and told me the details. He had been called to the scene where Roger's body was discovered on June 13 at 5 a.m. The police had blocked off the parking lot on the south-west corner of King and Jarvis. He had found Roger lying in the fetal position, his head cradled in his arm. He paused before making his assessment: Roger looked peaceful, like he was sleeping. There was no sign of foul play or altercation. A discarded needle and a tiny plastic bag with brown residue lay beside him. Dr. Gupta determined the death as an accidental overdose, pending the forensic report.

Dr. Gupta asked me about Roger. He said Roger appeared to have been overcome by the drugs in the syringe and had put his head down as if to sleep. He assured me that Roger's remains were treated with great care as he accompanied his body to the morgue for the autopsy.

I hung onto his words. His kind voice gave me a sense of peace. Roger was not bruised or battered. There had been no struggle. I scribbled down notes of the conversation. I couldn't trust my brain to retain any details. It would take a few months for the forensic report to confirm it had been a fentanyl poisoning.

It was Friday afternoon when Jill and I went to Turner and Porter, the funeral home in Bloor West Village, to make arrangements for the transfer of Roger's body. Roger, Brandon, and I had been there just months earlier for my friend Bill's funeral.

The funeral director welcomed us into the foyer. It was surreal to go through the motions. Numb with shock, I answered questions in my concierge mode, as if I was planning for some other family. Casket open or closed? Burial or cremation? I didn't have to decide right away. They assured me they would call the coroner's office and take care of all the arrangements. We left with a thick brochure full of options.

Jill put her arm around my shoulder as we headed home. Our paths had taken us in different directions since our carefree days as waitresses at The Other Café, but we always kept in touch. She knew Roger as a baby in Toronto and had visited us in Hawaii when he was only five. She witnessed the hope we had for him when he returned to Toronto to start a new life in 2010.

Later that day, we took refuge on a walk down the Humber River behind my apartment. We had an easy bond in which silence was comfortable. I was still clutching the teddy bear she had given me as we sat in James Gardens nestled in the ravine. Fresh-cut grass and roses in full bloom shared their scent with other summer blossoms heavy in the air. Back home, the news of Roger's death had spread across email and Facebook. Condolences and messages of support were flooding in.

Later that night, my friend Lee joined us. We had met in 1984, days after Henry and I were married and were moving into a new bachelor apartment at Queen and Roncesvalles in Parkdale. It was a newly renovated building, and several tenants moved in on that same day in May. Henry met Lee first, in the stairwell, and told me that a beautiful girl was moving in upstairs. I simply needed to meet her. She was fine featured with soft blonde hair and a flair for fashion. All in one week, I married the love of my life and met a soulmate. I still have the pair of blue suede booties with polka dots that Lee sewed for Roger when he was born. Over the years, Lee continued to sew me up whenever I was falling apart. I was like an old patchwork doll, with broken threads and jumbled fabrics.

In more recent years, Lucy, Jill, and Lee had been there for me as I unravelled during the lows and highs of Roger's addiction, recovery, and relapses. Tonight, we reunited in the eye of the storm. I felt enveloped in their love and care.

When my friends left later that evening, I found myself alone for the first time since receiving the news of Roger's death. Numb and unable to sleep, I made a cup of tea and took my blanket onto the patio. I sat in my favourite chair, looking at the dark sky. Was Roger up there? I heard distant thunderclaps, though the air around remained eerily still. Flash! A forked streak of lightning shot across the sky, silhouetting the trees. I shook and took a deep breath. Another almighty thunderclap roared, closer and louder. The sky above heaved and burst into a torrent of rain. I grasped my cup tighter and watched this holy storm unfold. Was Roger's spirit transitioning, causing a stir in the heavens? I sat in awe, thinking of him.

I remembered his first day at the local Waikoloa elementary school. He had marched into class without a backward glance at me. When the teacher, Mrs. Perwinkler, asked his name, he announced, "I'm Roger The Famous." And famous he was in Waikoloa, Hawaii, a tight-knit village nestled in the low slopes of Mauna Kea, with majestic views of the volcano to the east and the eternity of the Pacific Ocean to the west.

A few years later, Brandon followed Roger into Mrs. Perwinkler's kindergarten class. He looked just like his brother, and Mrs. Perwinkler needed no introduction.

"You're Roger's little brother."

Brandon had a serene nature in contrast to Roger's high-energy temperament. They were like chalk and cheese, my mum would say, and she was right. Roger played the forward position in the local youth soccer league and usually had the lead part in after-school drama productions. He was fearless. My heart was always in my mouth as I ran after him.

"Roger, stop! Slow down!"

In one instance, when Jill was visiting us on the Big Island, we went to swim at the resort where I worked. No sooner had we neared the pool when splash! Roger threw himself into the deep end declaring, "Look at me!" before his head bobbed below the surface.

I was holding baby Brandon in my arms. Jill jumped into the pool fully clothed to grab Roger, and I watched his head go under for a second time. This would not be the first near heart attack my oldest boy would cause me.

One day, five years later, Roger's fearlessness saved our lives. We were on a snorkelling trip off the Kona coast. It was a clear day, the sea and sky met in a blue band of infinity. The new charter service offered us a free trip, a perk I received as a hotel concierge. It was a small group—me, the two boys and three Japanese tourists. The boat anchored off Kua Bay where the reef was pristine and teaming with turtles and tropical fish. We donned our snorkel gear and floated around the boat. Soon, the boys eyed the crescent white sands of Manini'owali Beach, set against black lava rock. They'd had enough snorkelling.

"Let's go to the beach!" Roger exclaimed.

"We're tired of swimming," echoed Brandon.

The clear ocean reflected the blue sky as a gentle swell pushed us toward the beach. A wee break would do us good, I thought. We paddled onto the shore like explorers from a voyaging canoe. The boys, in full pirate mode, began searching for treasure and gathering seashells.

The boat bobbed on its anchor close by. We waved, and I thought I saw someone wave back. A few sandcastles later, I looked up. The boat seemed to be drifting further away and my heart started to beat faster.

"Okay boys, let's go."

We waded back into the water, donning goggles, masks, and fins. The ocean swell pushed against us now, yet on the surface, it appeared calm as a lake. Waves broke offshore on the reef.

"Come on boys! Swim! We're almost there," I urged as we aimed for the boat.

Brandon started to flail. His mask filled with water, and he swiped it off. We were treading water now, going nowhere. Panic rose. It took all my energy not to sink. I waved to the boat, but no one saw us. The gulf was widening. Brandon clung to me, crying.

"Mum, I'm tired. I can't swim!" He wrapped his limbs around me like a monkey, arms clinging around my neck. I made a split decision and called to Roger.

"Roger, swim! Swim as fast as you can to the boat. Tell them we need help. Go, quick!"

He swam off, and my heart stopped. Would he make it? Would we make it? The beach receded and Roger swam out of my reach. I prayed to God.

An eternity of minutes passed before I saw the boat turn. A hand reached out and pulled Roger onboard. Then, a mate jumped into the water with his surfboard and shot towards us. He took Brandon onto the board and towed me behind on a life raft. In those minutes, our lives flashed before me. Now again, memories floated through my head as lightning flashed and thunder rolled.

I grasped my tea on the dry island of my patio. I couldn't save Roger now; we had no lifelines left.

Just as I was drowning in panic, my phone rang. It was my friend Lesley from Scotland.

"Lesley, Roger's gone." I cried.

"I'm here, I know. Breathe, Irene. I'm coming over." Her Scottish lilt soothed me until I came up for air.

Arrivals

Saturday, June 17, 2017

I woke in the wake of the storm still on the patio. A streaky sun rose above the Toronto skyline. Overnight, Brandon's flight had sped through the turbulence en route from Glasgow. Lucy drove me to the airport, where I found that Brandon's plane had been diverted to Montreal, causing a four-hour delay. I waited alone in the terminal as jubilant families welcome loved ones. I felt invisible in my pain. It hurt to breathe, but I had to stay strong for Brandon. Each time the doors of the Customs hall swung open with a new batch of travellers, my eyes scanned their luggage tags and I listened for Scottish accents.

Finally, Brandon appeared, accompanied by the wonderful Air Transat flight attendant who had flown with him from Glasgow. My family had arranged for him to be escorted throughout the flight, and now she handed him off to me. He looked ashen.

"Brandon!"

He towered over me as I reached up to hug him.

"I'm so sorry, Brandon."

"It's okay, Mum."

But it wasn't. We were adrift. There would be no mate with a surfboard coming to our rescue.

"Let's go home."

Brandon had lived through seven years of Roger's addiction. The waves of Roger's intermittent highs and frequent lows had been chaotic. We crashed with every relapse.

December 31, 2012

On New Year's Eve 2012, I stood at the Concierge podium of the Soho Metropolitan Hotel. The luxurious marble panelled lobby buzzed with the chatter of well-heeled guests. The golden keys on the lapels of my tailored grey suit signalled service excellence. I obliged, assisting guests with last minute near impossible requests for reservations and limousines. It was relentless. Smooth jazz music spilled from the lobby lounge, beckoning those who wanted to take the edge off with a cocktail or champagne. In the cafe across the lobby, an espresso machine sputtered and steamed with a steady flow of caffeine. The fixed smile on my face caused my jaw to ache. It was 2 p.m.—one more hour to go.

My cell phone vibrated under the stack of papers on my desk. I shot a glance at the screen. "Where are you, Mum?" Roger's text was a flash of hope—he had gone off my radar since before Christmas.

I excused myself and took refuge in the baggage storage area in the back lobby—a windowless room lined with metal shelves heaving with parcels and expensive luggage. The phone shook in my hand as I sat in the spare wheelchair. I texted frantically; afraid I'd lost him.

"Roger, I'm at work. I'll be off soon. Where are you? I'll come and get you."

"I'm at Wellesley and Yonge. I'm hungry." he said.

"Go to the Starbucks near the subway. I'll meet you there."

Tears brimmed over my eyes and washed mascara down my cheeks. Was it too early to dim the glittering lobby lights to give me cover? My stomach heaved.

Back at the desk, I endured the last aching hour of my shift. Normally, I thrived on the adrenalin of busy days, but not today. The holiday spirit escaped me. My frazzled brain could think only of Roger. I looked up to see the welcome sight of my colleague walking towards me. He was tall and dapper in his impeccable grey suit and tie, not a hair out of place.

"It's good to see you, Xavier," I said.

I wanted this shift exchange to be brief.

"How was your day, Irene?" His French accent always cheered me, but I wanted to escape. I couldn't trust my voice to hold up.

"Good, very good." I said, avoiding eye contact. We went over the checklist.

"I have to run! Happy New Year!"

Panic engulfed me as I rushed up University Avenue against the flow of pedestrians pouring out of office towers. It was mild for December 31, above freezing. Early revelers packed the Nathan Phillips Square ice rink, skating in circles to piped-in holiday music. The Christmas tree sparkled in the background. I wept.

Cutting across to Yonge Street, I crushed into the subway northbound. The carriage was standing room only. Everyone looked like they had a plan for New Year's Eve. Teenagers laughed. Shoppers, discharged from the Eaton Centre, held their packages close. I held my breath. Could anyone see my fear? A few stops later, I was at Wellesley. Would Roger be there? I checked my phone; it had gone silent.

I pushed into the Starbucks, straining my neck to find him. He sat by the back window. His head bent, his long black hair matted over his face. I tried to wipe the shock from my face as I went to him.

"Roger," I smiled.

He lifted his head, but his glazed almond eyes avoided mine.

"Aww Roger … I'm here." I shifted onto the bench beside him.

"Mother, I'm starving," his straggled voice and mannerisms were foreign to me.

He never called me "Mother". I was always Mum.

I tried to normalize the situation, mum and son having a latte before ringing in the New Year.

"Let's go get something to eat. Would you like a burger?"

I put my arm around him and eased him out of the coffee shop. I felt the stares from the coffee drinkers, who stood shoulder to shoulder.

Roger and I walked south on Yonge Street as I held his arm. Even bent over, he towered above me. He wore layers of old jackets on top of a fleece shirt. I looked down and saw mismatched runners—no socks. I tightened my grip on his arm for fear he would bolt. There was a discount shoe shop on the east side of the street, and I steered him inside. The alarmed clerk sized us up with a look that said he'd call the police. I pointed to a pair of tan, heavy-duty lace-up work boots.

"We'll try a size ten please, and two pairs of socks."

Mercifully, we were the only people in the store. Roger sat down, swaying. He peeled off the odd, wet sneakers, and I saw his feet, swollen and red. I gave him the new socks with as much of a smile as I could muster.

"Put them on, Roger. You'll feel better." As if socks and shoes could salve his soul.

I handed the clerk my credit card. "He'll wear them," I said.

"Give me my shoes!" Roger yelled as the clerk removed his old ones.

"Put them in a bag, please," I asked, praying to leave without any commotion.

We walked south another block. Roger slammed the plastic bag holding his old shoes against a shop window. I thanked God the window didn't shatter. He ranted at passers-by. "What's up, bro? Let's party!"

"Look, there's an A&W!" I tried to divert him.

The orange sign lit up the corner. Roger ranted. It scared me that someone might take umbrage at him and start a fight.

"C'mon Roger! You said you were hungry. Let's get a burger."

We ducked inside. For a moment, the fluorescent lights blinded me.

"Sit over there while I order."

I pointed to an empty table against the wall. As I waited in line, I saw him put his arms out on the Formica table and drop his head. I felt the invisible cord that connected us tighten around my heart. I couldn't breathe as I squeaked out my order for two Teen Burgers, fries, and frosted mugs of root beer. My mind flashed back to the days of Happy Meals, when my boys were young.

"Roger ... here you go. Try to eat, son."

He was spewing gibberish at me—a psychotic break. His brain was on fire, in active addiction. What was he on? Was he detoxing? If he wandered into the night, what would happen? Would he make it through to 2013?

"Roger, I'm going to the washroom. I'll be right back."

Inside the cavernous single-use toilet, I gripped the porcelain sink with both hands to steady myself. I looked in the mirror at my ghostly reflection.

"Dear God, help us! What can I do?" I prayed. In desperation, I called the crisis line.

"Help! We need help! My son is sick. He's taken drugs ... he's out of his mind."

"Ma'am ... calm down. Where are you?"

"The A&W restaurant south of Wellesley and Yonge."

"Name please? Your son's name? Date of birth?"

"Irene. Roger Wong. October 31, 1988. I'm scared. I don't know what to do. We need crisis help."

"Ma'am, help is on the way. Stay there. Is this your cell phone number?"

"Yes, I ... help please." I shook as the phone line went dead.

I struggled to open the heavy bathroom door. Roger was now slumped over the table, disoriented. His leg thumped up and down.

"Roger, it's gonna be okay. Help is coming." I whispered.

He raised his head, sensing the shift.

"Mum?" It was the voice of five-year-old Roger, pleading.

If only it was a bloodied knee that a Band-Aid and a kiss could heal.

"Don't worry, Roger. It'll be all right."

Blue and red flashing lights lit up the window.

"Mum!" he screamed.

My phone rang. I grabbed it to my ear. "Step outside and identify yourself!" the operator on the line said. "This is emergency service."

Roger pushed away from the table and staggered to the bathroom.

I lifted the heavy glass mugs and placed them to the side as the other diners pressed against the walls. I walked to the door where two tall police officers in flak jackets advanced towards me. A paramedic stood by their side wearing a long white jacket with a stethoscope around his neck. He wore blue rubber gloves.

"Identify yourself!" one officer said.

"I'm his mum, Irene! He's sick!"

"Where is he?"

I motioned to the bathroom. They advanced.

"Don't! Let me get him! Please!" I had entered an alternate universe.

"Roger! Son! Come on out!" I knocked on the locked door.

An eternity passed in two minutes. Then I heard the lock click. The door opened and Roger shuffled toward me in his new boots.

"Mum?"

"Hands up! You're under arrest!"

I swung around as the police reached for him.

"You've got to help him," I pleaded to the medic.

"It's out of my hands," he shrugged.

Roger had no energy to resist as the police handcuffed his arms behind his back. He could barely stand up.

"What are you doing to my boy?"

"Ma'am, there's a warrant out for his arrest," the first officer said.

"For what?"

"Failure to appear."

"Appear for what?" I wanted to scream.

Roger lifted his head and stared at me accusingly. "How could you do this to me, Mum?"

The pain in his eyes burned into my soul.

"I'm sorry ... I didn't know."

They hustled him outside and into the back of a waiting patrol car.

"Stop! Where are you taking him?" my voice trailed as the police and emergency services vehicles sped off.

I looked back at our table, the burgers left uneaten, too shattered to cry. I staggered in shock down Yonge Street to the bus station. Somehow I made it home. On TV, I watched the ball drop for New Year's as I composed imploring emails to court support services and CAMH for intervention. I held onto the fact that Roger was alive, in custody. In the morning I was back at the concierge desk, smiling and pretending all was well as I rearranged my schedule to attend the court hearing.

This was one of the many traumatic events in the cycle of Roger's illness with addiction since he joined us in Toronto in 2010. I tried to protect Brandon from the chaos. The boys had a fraught relationship during these times, but nothing could prepare Brandon for losing his brother.

Back at the apartment, I boiled the kettle for a cup of tea, a pause to absorb our loss. Brandon lay on the sofa, exhausted. I covered him with a blanket and sat by his feet. We wept and slept fitfully.

Many others followed Brandon's arrival. That afternoon, Jenifer, aunty Jen, arrived—Brandon's godmother. She was a Minnesotan girl who could change a car engine then perform a hula dance with the grace of an angel. We had met in Key West even before I met Henry. She was a surrogate mum to the boys growing up in Hawaii.

When Roger was a baby, we vacationed in Hawaii to visit Jenifer. She introduced Henry, who was a chef, to a friend at the Hyatt Waikoloa Village hotel. Henry was hired on the spot and so began our island life. We had attained our green cards and had completed our immigration. After leaving the frigid north, Hawaii was a sublime spot to spend our first winter in the US. A winter that would last a lifetime. When I called Jen with the news of Roger's death, she said without hesitation, "I'm on my way."

She, too, was heartbroken, but her higher power was an ability to shepherd us through this crisis. The first thing she did was manage the phone calls and texts. It was hard for me to reply to questions I had no answers for. What happened? How? When? Why? Jen fielded them all. Like a Menuhune, she cleaned my apartment from top to bottom to prepare for visitors. She stocked the fridge with every imaginable snack, sandwich fixing, meal, and refreshment, including wine. We had once worked together as butlers at the Hapuna Beach Resort, and she knew how to organize any occasion. Funerals had not been in our repertoire to date, but Jen persevered.

Monday, June 19, 2017

Morning dawned with a cloudless sky. Jen and I had slept holding hands, knowing the day to come would not be an easy one. The coroner's office had released Roger's body to the funeral home—we could go ahead with the arrangements.

I received an unexpected email from a family friend:

> "Hello Irene, I just got back from Helen's and she tells me you are making arrangements at Turner and Porter tomorrow. I don't wish to intrude, but I can't bear to think of you suffering a financial burden on top of this terrible tragedy. I can meet you there or meet you afterwards. Just let me know. xo, Diane"

Brandon, Jen, and me—three broken musketeers—met Diane at a coffee shop in Bloor West Village across from the Turner and Porter Funeral Home. She was sitting on the patio, her red hair glinting in the warm sunshine. I introduced her to Jen, and we shared coffee and condolences. She passed a white envelope to me and said, "Take this. Bill wouldn't want you to bear any financial burden on top of the pain."

Bill was my Scottish friend who had run an Antique Store. He had adopted Henry and me when we first married in 1984 and moved to the Parkdale neighbourhood. We had wandered into his store, and the minute he heard my Glasgow accent, we bonded like long-lost clansmen. Abbey Antiques was located across from our apartment on Queen Street West. There, along with friendship, we found an eclectic mix of antiques and bric-à-brac to furnish our new apartment.

Years later, Bill welcomed Roger as a newborn and didn't mind me shuffling my pram through the busy store to sit and chat and share coffee. After we immigrated to the US when Roger was a year old, we kept up our friendship by sending letters and pictures. Bill displayed our snapshots from Hawaii on the store's curio cabinet and he loved the loud Hawaiian shirts we brought him when we returned to visit. It was Bill who gave Roger his first skateboard, called Big Red. Just seven years old at the time, Roger loved it. When I took the boys to visit Bill in hospice, Bill's last words to Roger were, "Look after your mum."

I prayed to him now, *"Aww Bill, I'm so sorry, Roger's gone. Perhaps he's with you, skateboarding in the big beyond."*

Diane handled Bill's estate. When he passed, he bequeathed me an Apple Macintosh computer. I had promised him I would write my story. Back then, the working title was, *It's Not the End of the World*—stories of my travels and tribulations. Now my world had ended, and Diane extended her helping hand to me. I gasped when I opened the envelope and saw a cheque "to cover the arrangements." I hadn't even thought of the cost of what I was facing, and now, this act of kindness lifted a burden I hadn't yet assumed. My broken heart absorbed their love and kindness. There was a God.

After coffee, we crossed the street to the funeral office, armed with the knowledge we could afford to make choices from the array of options. I was grateful to have Brandon by my side. He took charge, choosing the casket, the brass urn, and a visitor book for the memorial. We decided on a cremation with a private family viewing prior. This would allow Henry and Brandon an opportunity to see Roger one last time. We arranged the public service in the chapel for family and friends for Monday, June 26.

"Have you thought about the obituary?" the solemn funeral director asked. "Roger's memorial page will be posted on our website for family and friends to view."

"Yes, I'll email it to you," I said.

On the night of the storm, I had scribbled a rough draft. Roger's friend Caro edited it and added the last sentence, "He was fiercely loved, and will be deeply missed by all of us." The words are etched in my heart.

Next, Jenifer, Brandon, and I went to TD Bank on Bloor Street. The funeral director had given us a to-do list that included taking care of "Roger's estate." At least I could close his account at the bank and take care of his debts. One of the managers took us upstairs to her office and checked Roger's accounts. To our surprise, Roger had money in the bank—$2,000—he had been working and saving during his latest recovery. She explained that while we couldn't withdraw cash from his account, his funds could be used to cover any bills he had.

In my hand, I had the funeral invoice in Roger's name. Stunned, I handed it to her, and she made a bank draft out to Turner and Porter. With this, she closed his accounts. I felt Roger's hand on my shoulder and heard his voice in my head: *"Don't worry, Mum, it's gonna be okay."*

We returned to the funeral home and used Roger's bank draft to pay the deposit for his memorial service. Previously, we had declined the flower option to save money. Now, we chose a flower package with a wreath and two grand arrangements of white roses and lilies. The following day, Roger's obituary and funeral arrangements were posted on Turner and Porter's website.

In Celebration of
ROGER WONG

October 31, 1988 – June 13, 2017

Although Roger was born in Toronto, his family moved to the Big Island of Hawaii when he was a baby. He grew up in Waikoloa, a local boy full of Aloha. He was nicknamed "Roger the Famous" in kindergarten—a title that became him.

Roger's charismatic personality, beautiful smile, and warm heart won him steadfast love and friendship every step of the way.

His return to Toronto was during a challenging period in his life; it was here that his journey with recovery from addictions began. Roger came to know true joy in recovery, but ultimately the disease of addiction overcame him.

His mother Irene, his father Henry, his younger brother Brandon, all of his Scottish and Chinese relatives, his Hawaiian Ohana, and his adopted family and friends in recovery cherished him.

He was fiercely loved and will be deeply missed by all of us.

This was the first public verification of Roger's death, and it numbed me. Arrangements seemed to be moving at warp speed while I was stuck in quicksand. I don't know what I would have done without Jenifer. In the days leading up to the funeral, when I could barely string a sentence together, she choreographed arrivals and sleeping arrangements. Henry flew in from Hawaii with a stop in Florida to pick up his girlfriend. He said he needed her support. I understood, but felt Brandon needed our united support above all.

My apartment overflowed. My sister-in-law, Loraine, and my niece, Leann, arrived from Glasgow and were given the spare bedroom. Jen, Lorraine, Lesley, and I shared my bedroom while Brandon took the couch in the living room. Lorraine, with her beautiful head of curly blonde hair and razor-sharp wit, was my childhood friend. We had gone to middle-school in Glasgow together, graduated, and met Lesley at Langside College. As teenagers, Lesley and I had hitch-hiked fearlessly across Europe; Lorraine and I survived the Turkish invasion of Greece in 1974 by dancing the night away in a gay disco in Mykonos, oblivious to the impending war or the battles of life that lay ahead.

"Who do you think you are, getting a real bed?" Lorraine and Lesley quipped from the mattresses on the floor.

"First come, first served," Jen laughed as she bounced into the big bed with me.

There was laughter amid the tears as we shared stories into the wee hours of those long nights before the funeral.

Jen delegated tasks to me that I could handle. I compiled the music playlist for the memorial service. It included a mixture of Hawaiian tunes and Roger's favourite songs. Henry requested Brother Iz's "Somewhere Over the Rainbow." Every lyric held a new meaning to me now that Roger was gone. As I listened to Sting's "How Fragile We Are", and Kealii Reichel's "Goodbye My Friend" my grief flowed in tears onto the keyboard.

My other task was to create a photo collage. I searched through a lifetime of snapshots—Roger, a smiling, chubby baby; his first birthday, his wee face covered in chocolate cake as he pushed his Fisher Price bus. There was his Kindergarten graduation, a group shot of the keikis in bright aloha shirts with leis around their necks singing:

Love is something if you give it away,

Give it away, give it away.

Love is something if you give it away,

You end up having more.

There were also the daredevil shots of Roger catching a wave or doing a kick-flip on his skateboard. And so many Hallowe'en photos of his birthday celebrations through the years.

One by one, I saved the pictures to a thumb drive. Later, Jen and I went to the photo department at Wal-Mart to get them developed. Again, I relived the milestones of Roger's life as the photos flashed on the screen at the automatic photo booth. Click, size, save to the basket, again and again. My heart swelled as Roger came alive in the replays. Then my throat constricted, and I thought I would pass out as the photos developed before my eyes. They dropped one by one into the bin until the last one fell. I gasped, then broke into hysterical laughter—that last one, a black-and-white photo of a skinny dog in a bathtub, raggedy and lathered up with shampoo, its wee eyes bulging. Where did it come from?

The caption read, "It's been a rough week, but I made it … How about you?"

Jen looked over my shoulder in disbelief. There was no explanation. I didn't save that photo. Was it a sign from Roger, his cheeky self, reminding me to laugh? It had been a rough week. He had made it to the beyond; would I make it to the funeral?

Carpet Diem

May 2017

"Where are you, Mum?" My phone lit up with a text from Roger.

This new day held so much promise as the May sun slanted through the bus window. One more stop and I would be home. I knew where Roger was. My face could barely contain my smile.

"I'm almost there." I shot back.

Off the bus, I ran and skipped to the apartment.

It was Mother's Day, and my gift, my son, was waiting for me with a smile. His long black hair tied back in a ponytail showed his brown eyes framed in a sun-tanned face. He'd put on a few pounds and looked smart in his best jeans and buttoned shirt. My heart melted.

"Mum, I have a surprise for you. Close your eyes. I'll tell you when to open them!"

He shooed me into the bedroom to wait for the unveiling. I heard the table scrape across the parquet floor. What could it be? I felt like a child at Christmas. Now it was my child, a grown lad of twenty-eight, preparing the surprise.

"You can come in now. Open your eyes," his voice overflowed with excitement.

Roger was sitting in the big comfy seat by the window, an expectant grin on his face. The afternoon sun backlit the living room, and there, on the living room floor, was a rug. Not any old rug—a magic carpet.

I whooped and cried as I threw myself onto its soft pile, crisscrossed with a harlequin pattern of sea blue and ocean-foam grey.

"Roger! It's the beautiful rug, the one I saw at the Home Show!"

He laughed and joined me on the floor. I lay on my back and flung my arms ups.

"Do you like it, Mum?"

"Do I like it? Roger, it's the most beautiful thing I've ever seen."

He hugged me and handed me an envelope.

"Open it."

With an Academy Awards flourish, I tore open the envelope and pulled out a card. It was pink and fancy, emblazoned with flowers: A Mum Grows More Precious as Time Goes By!

Inside, he had written in his childlike scroll:

> "Mum, thank you so much for being there for me through my ups and downs. I would not still be here if not for you. I hope you like your gift and smile every day when you see it ☺. I Love You, Roger xxx."

"Aww, Roger."

We hugged outstretched on the carpet, an island of sunshine on my otherwise bare floor.

Only a month earlier, Roger had been working at the rug booth in the Better Living Centre. He was so excited to invite me to the Home Show, part of the Canada Blooms festival. I spotted him across the crowds, tall and dapper in a blue-and-red check shirt with dark dress pants. He radiated happiness as he smiled and hugged me. How proud he was to show off the array of beautiful woven tapestries hanging like works of art.

"Mum, if you could have one, which would you pick?"

They were all lovely, but I kept coming back to the blue and grey one. It reminded me of the Big Island of Hawaii, where he grew up.

"In my dreams, Roger, this is the one."

His eyes lit up as he shot me a toothy smile. He agreed it was his favourite, too. He was a charismatic salesman, animated and engaged. I was so proud of him.

A day like this might seem unremarkable for some, but for us, it was nothing less than a miracle. Spring was here, Roger was beside me, and I could breathe again.

This was his first job after completing rehab. He was in recovery at Alpha House and rebuilding his life. Only five months earlier, I had picked him up from downtown, where he was destitute and scared. The disease of opioid addiction was destroying him. It was freezing rain that November morning and he had spent the night on the street, panhandling in the Entertainment District. He told me later that a well-dressed man leaving a club saw him shivering on the sidewalk stoop and sat down beside him. They talked about family and the stranger reached into his pocket and gave him ten dollars, saying, "Watch yourself, brother."

That stranger's kindness gave Roger a lifeline to connect with me. Somehow, he made it to a twenty-four-hour Internet cafe on Yonge Street and logged onto a computer.

"Mum, come get me."

"Where are you, Roger?"

Those dark days seemed so far behind us now, as we hugged on the rug this Mother's Day—a gift given with such beautiful intention and love.

"…smile every day when you see it, Mum."

I do smile every time I see it. I smile and think of Roger. I cry, as well. In my mind's eye, I see him sitting on that island of azure-blue wool. But he's not there. A short month after our beautiful Mother's Day together, he died.

In his Narcotics Anonymous book, Roger highlighted this sentence with a yellow marker:

"As long as the ties that bind us together are stronger than those that would tear us apart, all will be well." The ties that bind us together are as strong and infinite as the threads in our magic carpet.

How Fragile We Are

June 26, 2017

The morning of the funeral dawned, the sky dark with clouds. We congregated in my small living room, spilling onto the balcony for air. It was stifling hot. At a casual glance, Brandon, in his black suit, and me in a simple black dress, looked like well-heeled patrons off to the theatre. In reality, we had stepped into a Greek tragedy. My role: Mother of the Deceased. I hadn't rehearsed for this. There was no script.

A chorus of friends and family from around the world arrived. Our supporting cast was in the wings. It was time to honour Roger and say our goodbyes.

"Are you ready?" Jenifer asked. The cars were waiting.

Our cavalcade drove to the chapel as a steamy rain fell. Inside, a garland of white flowers draped the altar. Two large tropical arrangements of orchids and birds of paradise flanked either side of the bronze urn that held Roger's ashes. Beside it, I placed a framed photo of him taken only weeks earlier outside of Alpha House. His long black hair was tied back and a wide smile crinkled his eyes. He was dressed in his blue plaid shirt and jeans, giving the "shaka" sign.

Henry joined us. He draped Roger's urn in a kukui-nut lei from Hawaii. Our grief galvanized us.

Hawaiian music floated through the stark wood-panelled chapel. Above the altar, a stained-glass window diffused the scant light filtering through the clouds. The sacristy held the adornments of most world religions, interchangeable to fit the service. Our Catholic priest waited while the funeral director dusted the crucifix and laid it on the altar.

A procession of family and friends arrived, making their way down the aisle to where Henry and I waited to greet them, one hug at a time. Henry looked gaunt, his almond eyes puffed from tears and jet lag. His face was taut, his hair more salt than pepper.

The congregation swelled with Roger's recovery community of counsellors and friends. Every seat was occupied. Roger's charismatic personality, beautiful smile, and warm heart had won him steadfast love and friendship. His death reverberated throughout the recovery community. Vulnerable and struggling, they came up to pay their respects. I was awestruck by their courage and condolences.

The funeral director motioned to us that it was time to begin. We took our seats.

Kevin Amisson, Renascent Rehab's Sullivan House manager, delivered the eulogy. It was no solemn soliloquy. He spoke from the heart, telling the story of the first time he met Roger. When he entered the recovery program, he was unresponsive and shut down, almost mute. He pushed the limits of participation, refusing to get out of bed and attend sessions. Kevin's wife, Heather, a family counsellor, had been my first contact with Renascent many years before. She knew my desperation and told Kevin then, "You've got to help this boy."

The counsellors persevered with Roger, pulling him from despair into recovery. Kevin told of an ah-ha moment he had after Roger graduated. On a sunny summer day, he had pulled into the parking lot of a local Wendy's fast-food restaurant. He thought of Roger and wondered how he was doing. As he glanced up, Roger was approaching his car with a bright smile.

"Wassup up, Kevin?" said Roger,

"Roger!" Kevin said he had pinched himself. That day, Roger was the poster-boy for recovery.

In his raconteur style, Kevin told of the impact Roger had made on him. He worked on the front lines of addiction, yet Roger had penetrated his armour. We all smiled and cried. Anyone who knew Roger could attest to the profound effect he had on others. He left his mark on your heart.

I saw the priest's expression soften as he sat with his hands clasped in the folds of his robes. This wasn't his usual Sunday audience. He proceeded with the service, tempering the holier-than-thou approach, and spoke instead of God's love and acceptance. He gave his final blessing, extolling, "Peace be with you."

A lone bagpiper strode towards the altar. The skirl of "Amazing Grace" reverberated up to the rafters, shaking the timbers and every nerve in my body. I draped my arms in a soft, cream-coloured blanket to receive Roger's ashes. The piper led the procession out of the chapel to the sounds of my homeland.

The cars arrived, and we set off amid a rainstorm to the community room of Lucy's condo. It takes a village, and Jill, Jenifer, and Lucy had transformed the space, giving it a comfortable ambience. The banquet tables, draped in tablecloths, held an assortment of sandwiches, salads and cookies. The kitchen was stocked with tea, coffee and soft drinks.

We placed Roger's urn on the mirrored armoire covered in white flowers. His friends laid their skateboards beneath it.

When the buffet was over, a calm came over the room. The sun dipped below the clouds in the west and shone through the lace curtains catching the dust motes as they danced in the glow.

I stood up to thank everyone for coming and shared the story of me developing the photos. I passed out a photo card Lee had made, and centred on it was the wee dog smiling in the midst of Roger's pictures.

"It's been a rough week, but I made it… how about you?" I said.

I felt a collective exhale.

"Would anyone like to share a word about Roger?" I asked.

One by one Roger's friends stood up and shared a memory of him:

"My name is… I first met Roger at a meeting. I was afraid to enter. He spoke with me and said, 'Come on in, it's OK.' I'm going to miss him."

"My name is…and I knew Roger in Oshawa. We were roommates and best friends. He helped me through some rough times."

"My name is…and Roger was my bro'. He was always there for me. I loved him."

Roger was alive in the testimonies of his friends.

As the last speaker began, a sweet baby, who had sat quietly on the rug, found her legs and stood up. She tottered, arms flailing, one step then two towards her mum. There was a gasp. The young couple cried. It was their baby's first steps.

It would take baby steps for us all to move forward from this day.

No One Ever is to Blame

July 12, 2017

The mailbox lock jiggled as I turned the key. It was July and the steady flow of sympathy cards had abated. I reached in and touched a bubble-pack envelope and pulled it out. The familiar British stamps heralded a package from my family in Glasgow. My heart raced in anticipation and trepidation. I knew without opening it what was inside.

In May, I had been to Glasgow for my niece Michelle's wedding, the youngest of my sister's five girls. It had been a happy visit shadowed by previous trips for funerals—my mum in 2015 and my sister Anne Marie in 2010—losses that broke my heart and left me with an ache unmatched until now. During the visit, my niece Irene had uncovered an old VHS tape labelled "Roger's 1st Year", which I had mailed to my sister in 1989. With the rush of wedding preparations, we'd had no time to watch it then.

"Aunty, I know a video store where we can get this copied to a DVD for you to take home," Irene had said.

"Great, Roger will love to see it." I smiled at the thought of sharing his first year on video with him.

The copy wasn't ready when I left, but she promised to mail it, and now I held it in my hands. Within seconds, I felt a familiar anxiety rise through my body. My legs shook, my stomach churned, my heart raced and pumped tears through my eyes. I squinted left and right in the cavernous lobby, thankful there were no witnesses to my breakdown. I escaped into the empty box of the elevator, slumped against the wall, and pressed the button for the fourth floor. Inside the apartment, I walked over our carpet to the desk. My hands shook as I cut through the bubble pack, a c-section to deliver Roger's first year.

On the cover was a picture of baby Roger in the arms of Libor, Lucy's husband.

I slipped the DVD into my computer and it whirred into play mode. The first scene flickered to life. As I watched, I felt transported back in time—as real as if I was living it all over again.

> I am cradling newborn Roger, all 6 lbs 7 oz, swaddled in a baby blanket against my chest, only his round head with a mop of black hair and wrinkled pink face visible. The bedside lamp casts a fuzzy orange glow. The voices of Libor and Lucy, my first visitors at St. Joseph's hospital on that evening of October 31, 1988, echo in the background. Libor is filming it all with his new camcorder.
>
> "He's got Henry's nose," Lucy says.
>
> "And his hair!" I reply.
>
> In my arms, I hold the most precious gift from God. We unwrap the swathing and check the baby's fingers and toes. I see Roger's little knees drawn up to his chest and his fist to his mouth.

Watching it, I'm returned to the moment of his birth. The pain of labour was no match for the agony of losing him.

> The next scene is Christmas Day 1988. Our wee baby dressed in a red Santa suit is being passed around like a parcel. There's a lot of oohing and ahhing. It's chaos in the cramped living/dining/everything room of our attic apartment on King Street West. The bassinet and Christmas tree compete for space with the dinner table set in the middle of the room. Our Shih Tzu dog, Poo Chi, scoots in and out of the frame. Lucy and Libor are over for dinner, hence the video. Libor loved his camcorder, thank God.
>
> Henry looks handsome in a white shirt and jeans, his long black hair tied back and cheekbones pinched high from smiling as he rocks Roger. At thirty-three years old, he is the spitting image of Roger at twenty-eight. I look frazzled in my Eddie Bauer Fair Isle sweater. With no time for glamour, hairstyles, or makeup, my 1980s permed hair sprouts from my head in all directions.
>
> The video rolls forward to spring. Our roly-poly Roger is on his baby blanket, shaking his favourite rattle, his sausage arms and legs flailing.

He sees we're filming and smiles, all gums, into the camera. His eyes folded between his chubby cheeks and forehead.

I'm singing along to Sharon Lois and Bram's: "Skinnamarinky dinky dink, Skinnamarinky do, I love you."

How we loved that one.

The grainy video moves on to summer, and Roger squeals with delight as he discovers the fun of his Fisher Price bus. When his chubby fist bangs the front of the bus, the roof flips up with a ring. He shrieks with laughter and thumps the bus again, each burst of surprise as genuine as the first.

Next, it is Roger's first birthday, Halloween 1989. We are back in the living room, more cramped than ever, with my toddler-group mums and wee ones. It's loud as the children go after the toys, treats and Poo Chi, who scurries away. Roger totters around in his OshKosh overalls.

"Ma, ma, ma," he mumbles as he pushes his Fisher Price baby walker. Three steps and plop! down he goes. He'd taken his first steps just weeks earlier. He pulls himself up, his chubby hands gripping the handle of the cart.

"Roger, you can do it!" I tell him to a round of applause.

Little Sophie in her party frills finds the Fisher Price bus, discarded now for the new birthday gift. Libor pans the camera to Lucy on the sofa who is cradling her new baby Paul—dear Paul who delivered a reading at Roger's memorial only weeks ago.

Watching the home movies, I saw how we had all settled into the bedlam of babies. Well, maybe not Poo Chi, poor dog. Watching the grainy images was mesmerizing. I forgot to breathe as the last scene showed Henry and me helping Roger blow out his first candle to a chorus of "happy birthday to you!"

The video rolled blank for a moment, then an old Much Music video from 1989 flickered onto the screen. I had copied the original home videos onto an old VHS tape.

Now Annie Lennox was singing, "Put a little love in your heart" from the movie *Scrooged*. It was one of Roger's favourite Christmas movies discovered in his teens. Annie's angelic voice poured from my computer like a message from God.

My pulse raced as I drew back from the vortex of all that had been beautiful in my life then. My baby, my husband Henry, and our friends—all together. I looked around my empty room for a witness. Sobbing, I picked up the phone and called Lucy.

"Lucy, remember the video Libor made of Roger's first year?" my voice broke. "I just received the DVD copy in the mail from my niece in Glasgow." I tried to breathe through my sobbing.

"I'll be right over, Irene."

In the background, the DVD played on.

Another Much Music video began, "No One is to Blame" by Howard Jones … "No one, no one, no one ever is to blame…"

I felt as if Roger was speaking to me from beyond. The hairs on the back of my neck stood up.

"Keep love in your heart, Mum. No one ever is to blame."

Did he know the "What ifs," and "If onlys" that paralyzed me now? I had picked him up when he fell trying to walk. I had picked him up many times during his battle with addiction. I had been there for him every step of the way, but the last steps he took to a parking lot in downtown Toronto were out of my reach.

"Put the kettle on," I heard my grandmother's voice in my mind. No matter the crisis, she always made a pot of tea. It was like a pause button, to catch a breath.

Lucy stepped through the door into the narrow kitchen, her arms opened in a hug. I put my head on her shoulder and wept.

"Lucy."

"It's okay, Irene."

We took our tea into the living room, where the shadow of Roger smiled from the big comfy chair by the window. The sun caught the colours in his carpet as we sat on the sofa.

"Lucy, I was supposed to show the DVD to Roger." The teacup trembled in my hand as I raised it to my mouth and gulped the hot tea over the lump that threatened to close my throat.

"I know, Irene. Let's say a prayer." Her voice steadied me as we said, "Our Father, who art in heaven, hallowed be thy name…"

Lucy shared my love for tea, and I shared her faith in Jesus. Prior to Roger's death, we had completed a ten-week course of "The Alpha Program" at our local All Saints Catholic Church. Each week over dinner, we delved deep into questions about the essentials of the Christian faith. Little did I know back then that faith, fellowship, and friendship would be the scaffolding that would hold me up.

After the balm of tea, we ventured over to my desk, and I once again pressed Play on the DVD player. Together, we relived the joy of Roger's first day and first year on earth through our tears.

My Return to Life

July 2017

My bereavement leave ended with a prescribed return-to-work date of July 10. It was barely a month since Roger's death. A shell of my former self put on a business suit and walked back into my job as a guest service manager at Minto, a luxury condominium residence in downtown Toronto. I hadn't crossed the threshold of that building since the day I ran out to go to the police station. The bellmen and concierge team greeted me with warmth and care.

"How are you, Irene?"

"We missed you."

"Welcome back."

Lights, camera, action. I smiled and nodded.

"Don't ask too much of yourself on your first day back, Irene," my director said as she walked me to my desk.

We barely knew each other. I had joined the management team with much enthusiasm only months earlier.

My desk was in the open reception area of the modern executive suite on the second floor. There was nowhere to hide from guests or colleagues. As I sat down, the memory of my last two days there overwhelmed me. It had been hell. Roger had stopped returning calls on Sunday, June 12. He didn't show up for the Blue Jays game on Tuesday and on Wednesday I'd sat paralyzed at that desk, refreshing my cell phone for texts, messages, calls—any evidence of his whereabouts. When I discovered he hadn't returned to his group home, I began to panic. I called his friends, his counsellor. I walked the streets looking for him. At 1 p.m. on Thursday, his friend Evonne met me at Minto. We walked out of the building to file the missing person's report.

Now, I sat there and shivered. The phone rang.

"How can I help you?" The cogs in my brain spun into automatic-pilot mode. This was what I did. I helped people. It was a skill I had honed over twenty years working in hospitality.

"Certainly, yes. I understand," I replied to the first complaint of the day. But I no longer related to the petty whims and discomforts of the guests; the housekeeper had missed a towel, the water pressure was low, the noise from neighbouring construction woke them up.

Did they not know people were dying on the street?

At home, I ate, but the food had lost its taste. It was only a means to keep my body and soul together. I stripped off my uniform and my armour, crawled into bed, and prayed. I had a plaque with the Serenity Prayer on my nightstand.

God grant me the serenity

to accept the things I cannot change;

courage to change the things I can;

and wisdom to know the difference.

I prayed to God and to Roger for peace. Like counting sheep, I recited any blessing I could find in the day; the bed I lay in, the roof over my head, Brandon and my family abroad, friends, a job that paid the rent. I pushed back at the pain with affirmations and lulled myself to sleep.

Then the nightmares began: I'm at work and Roger is trying to reach me. The phone on my desk rings. I shoot out my arm to pick up the receiver and the line goes dead. I run to another desk, where an enormous rotary phone stops ringing just as I grab the handset. Ten eyes glare at me from the round dial. Another phone rings in the adjacent office. I scramble through a maze of connecting rooms. Phones are ringing on every desk. I pick one up and a voice mocks, *"Press 9 for an outside line."* Clocks flash the time everywhere—wall clocks, desk clocks, alarm clocks. Tick-tock, tick-tock.

"Irene, can you see to that?" a vacant voice asks, as another folder is added to the pile on my desk.

The clocks tick and the phones ring, but no one is there. I'm all alone, shaking.

"It's Roger! He needs me!" I scream. *"Help!"*

My silent cry wakes me in a cold panic.

Sleep, my one escape, escaped me night after night. I fell deeper into terror. Day after day, I dressed and put on the mask: hair, make-up, smile. I rode the TTC downtown and walked through the doors to that desk. I projected an image of professionalism, but I was shattered inside.

One day, as I assisted a guest in her preparation for her son's arrival, she invited me into her suite. The smell of fresh-baked cookies filled the room. Her boy had graduated from high school and was now preparing to attend university.

"Would you like a cookie?" she asked, "it's his favourite."

"No, thank you," I smiled.

"Do you have any children?" She was making small talk.

"Yes." I looked at her kind face, mother to mother, and my heart raced.

"How many?"

Those two words punctured my heart.

"Um ... two ... ah ... one."

I edged backwards toward the door, cornered. The tears welled and broke free down my cheeks.

"Are you okay?"

I doubled over, my head turned away. I had no answer. I had two boys, but buried one.

"I'm sorry ... I don't know ... my son is ..."

She reached out her hand. I took it, breaking all professional protocol. My veneer cracked. We were just two mums.

"He's dead," I sobbed. "I have to go."

"Let's meet for a coffee away from here … when you're ready, Irene."

I knew she meant it and said, "Yes."

I escaped to the washroom and threw up. I dabbed my red eyes and powdered my face to conceal the pain.

"How can I help you?" was my mantra, but I couldn't help myself.

I reached out to Minto's Employee Assistance Program for mental health support and they assigned a counsellor. On my first visit, frightened and exhausted, I pressed the buzzer for entrance into a nondescript office. The waiting room was bland with cheap prints on the walls and year-old copies of *MacLean's* and *Toronto Life* strewn about. I flipped open a magazine and looked at the pictures. It trembled in my hands.

"Irene?"

I looked up to see Rosie. Sandals peeked out from below her flowing skirt matched with a flowery blouse. Her face looked small beneath wiry salt-and-pepper curls and black eyeglasses.

I willed a smile to my face.

"Come on in," she invited.

Her office was functional. A large window looked onto the roofs of Yorkville. Toronto highrises shimmered in the distance. A desk was in one corner and a bookshelf lined the other wall. Her chair faced a two-seat sofa padded with boho cushions. Between us, a small glass table with a box of tissues was at the ready.

Once she assured herself, with a battery of questions, that I wasn't an imminent danger to myself or others, Rosie cut the formalities and said, "Tell me, Irene, what brings you here?"

Words poured out of me like steam from an open spigot on a pressure cooker.

"Roger was doing so well … he didn't deserve … look at his picture … his smile … he's dead."

As my words flowed, Rosie made encouraging remarks in a soft voice, "Yes, go on."

I spoke and Rosie listened. In time I could construct full sentences to express my feelings. My recovery began like a twelve-step program: first, I admitted that my life was unmanageable and that I needed help. For years, my addiction was Roger's recovery. He was my life's purpose, and without him, my withdrawal was acute. There was no replacement therapy. Rosie gave me the space to unpack my grief.

Still, the nightmares continued. I'd wake with my heart heaving in the foggy quagmire at dawn. I would try to reassure myself: *"I'm in my bed. Breathe. It was a just a dream. Breathe."* Reality struck a harder blow. In the nightmare, there was hope that I'd reach a phone and hear Roger's voice, but in the cold light of day, the fact was clear that he would never call again.

As I shook awake, the cat lay across my chest. His weight counterbalanced my palpitations, and his purring pulled me from the abyss. Mr. Kitty needed to be fed.

Roger Memorial Art Contest

September 2017

In early September, Jordan, the manager of Alpha House, called. He was planning a Recovery Art Contest in memory of Roger. It was an honour to keep Roger's memory alive. Jordan sent me a copy of the poster and flyers to distribute. They featured an iconic photo of Roger taken outside Alpha House—smiling and making the shaka sign—the same photo we had used on his memorial card.

It read:

ALPHA HOUSE PRESENTS
ROGER WONG ART CONTEST

Are you in recovery or struggling with addiction?

We believe in you and want to showcase your talents to the world!

Submit your original artwork by September 30th and you could win the Roger Wong Award

and $250 in art supplies.

Submissions will be showcased in a recovery art show.

I wanted to help in any way I could and agreed to distribute the flyers. Roger's friend Evonne offered to join me. It was 3 p.m. and I was ground down from another workday running interference between guests and the renovation crew. My phone rang with complaints all day and by 2 p.m. I was exhausted. I should have gone home to bed, but I met Evonne in the coffee shop downstairs. We planned to pass out the flyers to a few rehab centres in the downtown core. I gulped a cup of strong coffee on an empty stomach, and we set off.

It was a warm afternoon, the early fall day clinging to summer. We made our way to Madison Avenue, a Renascent men's treatment centre near Spadina and Bloor formerly called Punanai. Roger had completed his third and last rehab there in January. In the foyer, I looked over to the familiar sitting area where a sofa and two armchairs were arranged around the fireplace. The afternoon sunlight shone through Venetian doors that led to the garden.

The counsellor, a well-dressed, soft-spoken man who looked about thirty, not much older than Roger, greeted us warmly. "How can I help you?" he asked.

I introduced myself and opened the folder to show him the flyer. Roger's smiling face gazed from the coloured page.

"Do you remember my son, Roger?" I asked. "He was here in rehab last Christmas. We're having an art contest in his memory."

In his memory, the words stuck in my brain. The blood drained from my face as I reached for the hall table to steady myself. I blinked as I looked into the sitting room. In my mind's eye, I saw Roger sitting on the sofa, the Christmas tree lit up behind him.

"Hi Mum, let's go for coffee," he smiled.

I wanted to reach over and hug him.

I shook my head. Roger's image was on the flyer in my hand. The couch was empty. There was no Christmas tree, no hope. I swallowed hard to suppress the terror rising in me. The counsellor took the flyers and said something I didn't hear.

"Can you pass them out? The deadline to submit is September 30," I stuttered.

Escape.

There was a parkette nearby, and I motioned to Evonne. We sat down. Trash stirred in the breeze around our feet.

"I'm sorry, I feel a bit of a headache coming on," I said.

I didn't share what had happened to me in the foyer, for fear that I was losing my mind.

We had one more stop to make at the women's rehab on Dundas Street. I changed into my flat pumps, red with brass buckles, hitched up my suit pants over my white eyelet cotton shirt, and slung my black jacket over my arm.

"Let's go."

I stuffed the folder of flyers into my bag and mustered some courage.

We walked along the north side of Dundas, dodging construction and crowds squeezed under the scaffolding. Monroe House, the women's treatment centre, was in a brick brownstone house across from the Art Gallery of Ontario. I rang the doorbell, and a counsellor came out onto the stoop.

She didn't invite us in; I handed her the flyers.

"Please, if you could distribute them, it's for an art contest in memory of Roger." I averted my eye from the flyer.

I remember little else of being there, only the rising panic within me. As we left, I realized the neighbourhood we were in, on the cusp of Chinatown, close to the police station. My head pounded.

"I don't feel well. Maybe we should eat. Are you hungry?" I asked Evonne, wondering if she was okay.

She nodded yes.

We went into a nearby noodle house, a cheap and cheerful hangout for university students. It was early yet, before the dinner rush. We sat by the window overlooking Dundas Street West. The nine-to-fivers streamed out of their offices like ants.

The waiter delivered our wonton soup and ramen noodles as we sipped jasmine tea. It warmed the chill in my veins, but jackhammers still pounded in my head. After a quick bite, we paid the bill and left. As we walked towards the subway, it loomed—the 52nd Division Police Station. I stopped, paralyzed. I never wanted to see that building again. I grabbed a lamppost as a wave of nausea flooded over me, then I retched. Tea, wontons, and what felt like my heart hurled out of my mouth, down my pants, over my shoes and onto the sidewalk. Bile shot up my nose and I gagged.

"Are you okay, Irene?" Evonne asked.

"No! Get a taxi." My throat burned. "I need to get home."

An unsuspecting cabby pulled over. He saw the state of me, but instead of hauling off, he passed me a plastic grocery bag.

"Where to?" he asked.

The cab merged into the rush hour away from the crime scene. I gripped the bag to my face and caught the driver's eyes in the rear-view mirror. He looked sorrowful, maybe at the thought of fumigating his taxi, or just concerned about me. He didn't ask questions other than the address we were going to. We arrived home in a blur of traffic.

I ran the gauntlet through the lobby, up the elevator, and down the corridor. My hand shook as I opened the door to the apartment. I dropped my bag and ran to the washroom. I turned the shower on full blast and stepped into the steam, retching. The spray washed over me as I stripped off my clothes, which fell in a puddle at my feet. My ribs ached as the dry heaves churned to a choking hiccup.

The thread of sanity that I had held on to was stretched like a bungee cord. I was falling.

Recovery Day

September 30, 2017

Each morning, I stuffed my panic into a mental drawer and dragged myself to work. Sunglasses hid my tears and invisible scars on my daily commute. For the past seven years I had lived a double life. I could make your day with the perfect reservation or sightseeing trip, while I planned interventions, scheduled detox, and kept track of probation appointments. Now, I was adrift. The fire of advocating for Roger's recovery had been extinguished.

Evonne told me about the Toronto Recovery Day and encouraged me to participate. It was held on September 30 at David Pecaut Square. The sun shone on the large concrete public space at the base of Metro Hall where The Eternal Flame of Hope burned nearby to remind us that society must be all-inclusive. Booths ringed the square with community partners: CAMH, Renascent, Oasis, and others who shared information about recovery and harm reduction programs. From a large stage, guest speakers amplified the message of awareness and hope for freedom from addiction.

I met Angie Hamilton, executive director of Families for Addiction Recovery (FAR), whose booth was near to the stage. A lawyer and advocate, she was self-assured and friendly, sporting a FAR logo t-shirt and a warm smile under curly brown hair. She had her son beside her, while all I had was a framed photograph of mine, shaking in my hand.

Stage-side was frantic. The organizers, recovery mavericks Lisa Simone and Annie McCullough, kept the program running while fielding press and media interviews. We checked in with the production assistant, who looked at her clipboard for our names. "You're up in thirty minutes."

This was my first time at a rally of any kind. Evonne had introduced me to the organizers and given me a beautiful poem to recite. I looked at Angie for reassurance. Our slots were one after the other, and she offered to come on stage with me.

We stood together as she delivered her message of families helping families and peer support while advocating for policy changes at the government level. I felt bolstered by her strength—we were two mums standing together for change. She introduced me as a mother who had lost a child, my cue to step forward to the microphone.

"Good afternoon. My name is Irene, and this is my son Roger." I held his picture above my head with both hands. "He died from a fentanyl poisoning, walking distance from this square. He was one of hundreds of loved ones who have died in the opioid crisis this year in Ontario. Please join me as we remember them. This is a call and response poem. Repeat with me, 'We Remember Them.'"

My voice began unsure and shaky, but gained momentum as I read:

> At the rising sun and at its going down;
>
> We remember them.
>
> At the blowing of the wind and in the chill of winter;
>
> We remember them.
>
> At the opening of the buds and in the rebirth of spring;
>
> We remember them.
>
> At the blueness of the skies and in the warmth of summer;
>
> We remember them.
>
> At the rustling of the leaves and in the beauty of the autumn;
>
> We remember them.
>
> At the beginning of the year and when it ends;
>
> We remember them.
>
> As long as we live, they too will live, for they are now a part of us as …

I heard the crowd repeat, "We remember them," and my voice quivered. I looked to Angie for reassurance; she nodded, and I continued,

When we are weary and in need of strength;

We remember them.

When we are lost and sick at heart;

We remember them.

When we have decisions that are difficult to make;

We remember them.

When we have joy we crave to share;

We remember them.

When we have achievements that are based on theirs;

We remember them.

For as long as we live, they too will live, for they are now
a part of us as,

We remember them.

The refrain, "We remember them," reverberated throughout the square. Goose-bumps prickled up my arms as I looked over the audience, young and old. For a moment, we were one big family with a common purpose—recovery. Angie smiled, put her arms around me, and guided me off the stage to my friends waiting in the wings—Caro, Sandra, Joan, Julie, Amy, and Evonne had all come out in support.

The event promoted harm reduction. Medical professionals demonstrated how to administer Naloxone, a life-saving medication used to block the effects of opioids and reverse an overdose. I took the training along with dozens of others and received a free kit. The small black zippered pouch emblazoned with NALOXONE in red letters included two doses. I could save a life, not Roger's, but, for a moment, I felt a spark of hope take seed. Advocacy entered the void in my heart.

The Salmon Run

Monday, October 9, 2017

Looking from my balcony towards the Humber Ravine, I saw the maple leaves curl, losing their lustre. Not yet falling, they clung to the early fall sunlight. I felt drawn to don my sneakers and venture out for a walk.

The speckled sunlight played with my eyes as I moved through the groves of trees along the riverbank. It heightened my senses, and I squinted to focus. Water rushed over the nearby weir on its downward flow to Lake Ontario. This, combined with the harmony of the wind in the trees and the birds chirping, was a symphony of nature. I smiled and stopped to soak it all in.

Then I heard a roar of voices and applause. A crowd clamoured by the riverside and I rushed over to see what the commotion was all about. A flash of silver glinted as a lone salmon propelled itself against the falling water.

"Wow!" I screamed and joined the chorus.

But the salmon didn't make it. It swerved below the falls, gathering momentum for another dash. Then another salmon leapt out of the water, flying three feet high. It landed in the calm, shallow waters above. Splash! We cheered and clapped.

"Yeah, you did it!" I yelled.

Children jumped up and down. Dogs yelped and ran in circles. The salmon run! I shifted my way to the front of the crowd and sat down, mesmerized, on the concrete ledge of the riverbank. I had a front-row seat to watch this concert of nature. My eyes, now adjusted, counted dozens of silvery warriors swirling in the shallows, each vying for its turn to join a primeval quest to dash upstream.

The sagging sun caught each fish in all its magnificence, glinting off their pearly scales. I held my breath at every leap and cheered them on their journey. We all celebrated in unison, each time one cleared the weir to the next level. I lamented at nature's callousness as the weaker ones beat themselves to exhaustion against the wall of water. Bloodied and battered, some never made it, floating belly-up in the foam.

I continued my walk. A mile further on was another weir. I realized those magnificent specimens who had made the first leap now faced their next hurdle: another ladder to climb before their spawning grounds. Where would they get the strength? Would they have given up at the first leap if they knew what was ahead?

I sat near a quiet part of the river where silver streaks of salmon swam in circles. I sobbed silently. How many would make it?

My mind turned to Roger's struggle with addiction. Every time he hit a wall and relapsed, he would rally to take another leap at life, not knowing what was ahead. He pushed forward while we cheered him on. We celebrated the calm waters of recovery while he gained his strength.

"You can do it!" his Ohana rallied for him again and again.

"Come on Roger, you can do it."

A Pain With a Name

October 11, 2017

Fall arrived with a fresh chill in the air. Pumpkins sprouted in grocery stands, and their ghoulish candlelit faces lurked in entranceways and windows. Roger, my wee pumpkin, was born on Hallowe'en. For the last twenty-eight years, it had been a celebration. Now, it was a mocking reminder of my loss.

I woke with a deep ache in the base of my spine. My skin prickled under the spray of the shower, and I noticed a bumpy rash across my shoulder and neck. I dressed to cover it up and prepared to go to work.

"You can do this, Irene," I told myself in the mirror.

I fought against the will to give up and prayed to God for help. It was a Friday. I just needed to get through the day.

Arriving at work, I greeted my team at the concierge desk. The lobby was spruced up for the season. Behind the desk I saw pumpkins. I swallowed hard—I felt my skin cringe. The morning began with the usual daily operations meeting in the boardroom, where department heads huddled around a large oval desk to discuss the business of the day: arrivals, departures, maintenance issues, and the renovation schedule. I tried to focus on the day's objectives, but all I could feel was the ache in the marrow of my spine. My skin was on fire. When the meeting was over, I couldn't stand up from the black leather chair. The management team dispersed, but I sat motionless. I couldn't pretend for another minute; my body and mind had broken down.

The director, a poised, blonde-haired woman in her fifties, noticed my distress. "Are you okay, Irene?"

"I'm sorry," I blurted, "I'm not well, look."

A red rash flamed up one side of my body and now covered my neck.

"Oh, Irene! Go to the doctor. We'll handle things here today."

She helped me get my coat and escorted me back through the lobby. I walked out with my head down and my collar up.

The cafés on Yorkville Avenue were full of people enjoying the remnants of summer. Well-heeled locals walked their fancy dogs in the cool sunshine. I walked in a daze to my doctor's office a few blocks away. The receptionist squeezed me in for an appointment with my GP, who was aware of Roger's passing. I slumped onto the chair in the sterile examination room, dressed in the gown the nurse gave me. As I waited, I memorized the eye chart on the wall.

The doctor flipped her auburn curls back as she walked into the room and took up her position at the desk next to me. The computer hummed when she logged on. "What brings you here today, Irene?" she asked in her perky way.

"I feel an awful pain right in my spine, and my skin is on fire. I'm exhausted."

"Look." I peeled back the robe.

She examined the rash that feathered across my chest on the left side and fanned up over my shoulder. I was running a slight fever.

"Irene, you have symptoms of Shingles." She showed me a diagram depicting the virus following meridians in the nervous system. The picture showed blisters on the skin. As horrific as it was, this pain had a name. The other pain I felt was invisible.

She turned back to her computer and printed a prescription for 50 mg Pristiq, an antidepressant.

"Go home and rest, Irene. Take these as prescribed and painkillers to ease the symptoms. The virus will run its course."

She returned to the computer and typed up an absence note for my workplace.

Physically and mentally, I was a mess, but my release from Minto let me exhale. I didn't have to pretend anymore. At home, I made a cup of tea, wrapped myself in a blanket, took the pills, and let go.

As the burning virus ran its course, I succumbed to pain and tiredness, giving up any expectations of myself. I woke, ate, and slept. Mr. Kitty was my alarm clock.

A quick scoop of dry food in his bowl was my snooze button. Pyjamas were my new uniform.

I was on short-term disability from work by the time October 31 arrived.

That night, Jill, Lucy, Sandra, and I went to Alpha House to be with Roger's friends. I felt close to him there. Together we celebrated his first heavenly birthday. This Ohana helped me over my aversion as we carved pumpkins together in his memory. We lit them with tea-lights and placed them outside. Orange beacons of love for him.

Let Go and Let God

November 1, 2017

Days passed until the laundry basket overflowed and the bag of cat food emptied. I ventured out to the common laundry room and across the street to the grocery store for supplies. For the last seven years, I had toiled and scraped by with my "it's-not-the-end-of-the-world" mantra, grasping at hope in every dark corner. Without Roger's recovery powering me, how could I continue living?

I sat at my window and stared over the Humber River ravine. The stalwart maple trees bent to the wind, dropping their crown of golden leaves.

The phone rang.

"Irene, can I pick you up for church on Sunday?" I stifled my tears when I heard Lucy's sweet English lilt.

She picked me up, literally and figuratively. A calm came over me as I sat beside her on the bench in All Saints' Church. The familiar scent of incense and wood polish filled the air as a cold November light streamed from the glass dome above us. Behind the altar was a statue of Jesus on the cross. I clung to the familiar rituals as I listened to the reading from the Book of Ezekiel 34:11: "As a shepherd tends his flock when he finds himself among his scattered sheep, so will I tend my sheep. I will rescue them from every place where they were scattered." I hung on every word.

The psalm for the day was Psalm 23. "The Lord is my shepherd; I shall not want." I gripped Lucy's hand—we had read it at Roger's memorial.

When the Mass was over, we visited the shrine of Mary the Holy Mother in the church foyer. The votive candle sputtered to life as I held a match to it. "*Mother of God, pray for me,*" I crossed myself and paused for a moment as the words of Eric Clapton's song "Holy Mother" rang in my head—a song he wrote in the depths of his addiction.

The candle flickered in its blue globe.

"I'm sorry, Roger. Mother of God, help me," I prayed under my breath.

Across the stone floor stood the statue of St. Theresa, my patron saint, holding an armful of roses. She vowed that, "as long as there were souls to be saved, she would let fall a shower of roses from heaven."

"Save my soul today. I failed my boy." I cried.

I found solace in the prayers and in Lucy's company. Our Sunday trips to Mass were recovery steps in my life after Roger.

Do Something Prime Minister

November 10, 2017

The Recovery Day rally had planted a seed of advocacy in my soul. I connected online to Angie's Families for Addiction Recovery and another group, Moms Stop the Harm (MSTH), a group of families whose loved ones had died from drug-related harms or who struggled with substance use. The magnitude of shattered families I found in this group was staggering, six hundred in BC alone. The courageous members of MSTH were united in advocacy. Even the name "Moms Stop the Harm" spoke to action beyond grief. I pored over posts from hundreds of families coast to coast. Pictures of loved ones lost, sons like my Roger, daughters, friends with smiling faces—all gone forever. There was comfort in knowing others related to the pain that even I couldn't fathom. I was far from alone in my grief.

In November 2017, MSTH launched the "Do Something Prime Minister Photo Campaign," a mass mailing to the Prime Minister from families who had lost loved ones in the opioid crisis. I printed out the instructions, which called for us to send either a photo of our loved one or a purple heart with their name, birth date, relationship, and cause of death.

Roger mattered. He was not a statistic. How could Prime Minister Trudeau ignore Roger's beautiful face and smiling eyes and not do something about the opioid crisis? I took the energy of my feverish grief and cleared the dining table. I chose the memorial card with Roger's picture, his name and date of birth and death embossed on the front. To this, I pasted a copy of the coroner's report, enlarging the section, "Cause of Death: Acute fentanyl and morphine intoxication." Next, I cut a chain of purple hearts and on each one I wrote the names of Roger's loved ones, beginning with me, his dad, brother, aunties, uncles, the loves of his life, and his friends. I wrote the MSTH slogan, "SOMEBODY'S SOMEONE," in capital letters with a purple marker around the outside of the envelope, along with "DO SOMETHING PRIME MINISTER". I addressed it, as directed, to the PM's office.

It was Monday, November 13 when I put the envelope in the mailbox. I hesitated before releasing my fingers to let it go; it contained my broken heart. Back home, I logged onto the MSTH forum. Hundreds of mums, just like me, had sent their photos too.

I felt another type of pain: stigma. Did we not matter? Any other illness or outbreak would be front-page news. Of the opioid crisis, we heard close to nothing. I raged inside. Did anyone care? I wanted to open the window and scream: *"My son is dead!"*

On the radio, I heard the familiar sound of the CBC news: "CBC, Canada Lives Here." Overcome with the injustice of it all, I Googled "contact the CBC" and found a link. I clicked onto their website and completed the pop-up form. It was easy enough: name, address, email, and the reason I wanted to contact them. I introduced myself as a mum who had lost a son to the opioid crisis in Toronto and explained the Do Something Prime Minister initiative. I asked if they would cover the story. Shivers ran through my body when I hit send. I pulled my cardigan tight around my shoulders. My private grief hurtled through the wires to the Canadian Broadcasting Corporation. What had I just done?

The antidepressants softened the edges of my brittle nerves, and the Shingles rash retreated slowly. The more I slept, the more I wanted to sleep, but my hermit life came to a screeching halt when the phone rang early on Saturday, November 18. It was a sunny morning, but my mind was in a fog when I grabbed my cell phone.

I didn't recognize the caller ID, so I used my best concierge voice. "Hello, Irene speaking."

"Irene, this is the CBC. Thanks for contacting us regarding Moms Stop the Harm and the photos to the Prime Minister. We'd like to do a piece for the National tonight. Would you be available for an interview with Lisa Xing?"

I was so nervous I could barely hear anything after "CBC". "Yes, it's Irene here … em … yes, I am."

"We'd like to send a crew to your home," the producer said.

"When?"

"Today, 1 p.m. … if that's okay with you … for the 6 p.m. broadcast."

I said yes and gave them my address in a daze. Then I realized I wasn't prepared for a camera crew. I called Jill.

"Jill, remember I sent Roger's picture to the Prime Minister? The CBC just called. They want to do a story, and they're sending a crew over here today at 1 p.m. Can you come over right away?"

"Don't worry Irene, I'll be right there."

I knew I'd better get out of my pyjamas. I peeled back the shower curtain and turned on the shower full blast; adrenalin ran through my body like the hot water in the pipes. I spoke to Roger from this steamy confessional booth: *"Roger, give me strength … what's happening?"*

I'd only just heard of Moms Stop the Harm. I was hardly a spokesperson. But I was a mum, and God knows, there was harm to be stopped. I ran into the kitchen wrapped in a towel, hair dripping wet. Dirty dishes were piled in the sink, and the living room was, well, lived in. I knew that it wasn't Home and Garden TV that was coming over, but the caller did say The National. With just a couple of hours to go, I whipped into action. I couldn't remember the last time I'd vacuumed. Mr. Kitty fled, fur flying under the bed. By the time Jill arrived with muffins and a smile, I was fluffing up the cushions on the old beige sofa.

"What can I do, Irene?" Jill gave me a big hug.

"Thanks for coming. Let's have some coffee for a start."

It steadied me to have Jill there as a friend and a witness—otherwise, I might wake up and find it was a dream. In hindsight, it was a blessing that I had no time to think. I had printed out the Moms Stop the Harm "Key Beliefs" for context. The sheet lay on the coffee table.

> Moms Stop the Harm calls for and supports:
> 1. Families as partners in finding solutions
> 2. Support don't punish—decriminalize personal possession of illicit substances
> 3. Saving lives through harm reduction
> 4. Redefine recovery
> 5. Ending the harm caused by bad drug policy

6. Know the drug, minimize the risk
7. Bereavement support

I could also quote the grim opioid-related deaths for Ontario in 2016: seven hundred and twenty-six. The numbers weren't out yet for 2017. I wasn't an expert on statistics. I was Roger's mum, one face of the epidemic. The face of one mortality.

"Jill, I'd better dry my hair and fix my face."

I looked into the mirror and saw a scared, pale reflection of myself. I brushed powder over my face but couldn't conceal the loss in my eyes. A bit of rouge on my cheeks made me look like a clown. I rubbed it off. I threw on a simple black sweater and pants. The last thing I wanted was to bring attention to myself.

"What do you think, Jill?"

"You're good. Don't worry, Irene. It will be okay."

"I'll light a candle. They'll be here soon."

I took a tea light to the shrine for Roger that I had created around the golden box of his ashes. His picture was propped up by the ornate bronze guardian angel with arms outstretched to cradle the candle. I reached for the lighter—Roger's BIC— pale pink with a tattooed design of butterflies and a small rose curling up the side. I remembered the day we had bought it at the corner convenience store near the rehab centre, when I visited last Christmas. We had walked down to the Second Cup for coffee. It had been a day of answered prayers. My boy was in recovery.

"Mum, can you buy me cigarettes?" I heard his voice in my mind. He needed a lighter and picked the BIC from the display on the counter. A transaction easily forgotten, but now, I felt Roger's hand on mine as I struck the flame to the wick. I lit the candle and dropped it into the holder. I had also kept the pack of BB Lights cigarettes he left in the drawer by the patio door. As if I expected him to waltz in at any moment and take his place on the balcony for a smoke. The ashtray was still out there.

Jill and I sat together on the sofa, sipping coffee. We stared at the clock, waiting for the buzzer to ring, yet jumped, startled, when it did. I opened the door to a petite woman dressed in a soft blue blouse and pants. She smiled.

"Irene, I'm Lisa from the CBC. This is John, my camera man."

"Come on in." I tried to sound natural, like this was an everyday occurrence.

John removed his shoes and unpacked the gear silently. I invited them into the newly fluffed living room. My mum would have been proud of me, God bless her soul. It was important to keep up appearances in our family.

They arranged the setting for the interview, moving my pair of old Queen Anne chairs to the centre of the room on Roger's carpet. John set up the camera and lights and began recording. We sat down, Jill off to the side for moral support. Lisa gently asked me about Roger; how old he was and the circumstances around his death, and the MSTH campaign.

"Irene, you sent Roger's picture to the Prime Minister. Can you tell me about that?"

I held out Roger's picture and spoke from my heart. The large collage we had made for Roger's memorial stood near the sofa—a kaleidoscope of his life from birth to our last night together. I watched John move the camera in for a close-up. I passed Lisa a recent summer picture taken of Roger, standing on the boardwalk at the Sifton Bog wetland park. We held the picture between us, frozen in the frame. In a flash, the camera caught my tears, my grief, my disbelief.

Lisa and John rushed off to file the story for the 6 p.m. CBC National news.

Later that day, Jill, Caro, and I went to celebrate Roger's best friend receiving his one-year abstinence medallion at a local Narcotics Anonymous meeting. Roger's recovery family was like Ohana to me. I had gone with Roger to many of his twelve-step meetings and saw him receive his own coveted medallions; twenty-four hours, thirty days and, on two occasions, one year. It was an honour and inspiration to be in the room and hear the stories of hope in recovery and the mantra, "Keep Coming Back." The last night we were together, Roger and I were supposed to attend, but dinner ran late and Roger had said he'd go the next day.

Back home alone, I turned on the TV for the 11 p.m. news. Roger's picture flashed across the screen.

Marivel Taruc began:

> "A mother is calling on the federal government to do
> more to stop the overdose crisis. That's after her son
> died of an overdose in June. She's joined a network

of Canadian families lobbying Ottawa. They're called Moms Stop the Harm. They're sending photos of their loved ones to the prime minister. Lisa Xing joins me on this now. So, Lisa, Toronto is certainly not immune to this epidemic."

"No, it certainly isn't," Lisa said. "This is a national issue, Marivel. Toronto police here say they have noticed a thirty percent increase in the number of overdose calls last month compared with October 2016. So, the mum I spoke with today says she wants the government to step in and help."

Again, Roger's smiling face appeared on the screen.

"That's Irene's son, Roger," said Lisa. "He would have turned twenty-nine in October, but back in June he was found dead in a parking lot in downtown Toronto from a fentanyl overdose."

The camera zoomed into my face, tears streaming down my cheeks.

"My life ended. How can that be? I just had sushi with him, I just saw him, he was doing so well." I was shaking.

"Roger had been six months drug free leading up to his death," Lisa continued, "a longer stretch of sobriety than most times before this relapse."

"We had tickets to go to the baseball game on Monday, and he didn't show up," I said. "He was supposed to meet me and he didn't show up. I called his friends and went to where he was staying and they said he went for cigarettes. He never came back."

The camera zoomed into Roger's memorial photo, the iconic shot of him standing by the wall at Alpha House, smiling with his hand raised in the shaka sign.

"To raise awareness of how devastating the overdose crisis is on loved ones," Lisa said, "Irene sent this portrait of Roger to Justin Trudeau as part of a nation-wide campaign lobbying the federal government to do more to get fentanyl off the streets. So far, more than five-hundred families have sent in photos."

The camera zoomed back to me in tears.

"Every day, you see the statistics and all of that, but I just thought if people could see what's left behind, the devastation of families and friends and loved ones. It's hard. Roger is gone. There's nothing I can do to bring him back, but I can help somebody else. Together we can help somebody else's someone."

"Now, Irene says that she wants people to have wider access to supervised consumption sites and have various ways to help those already addicted, and then she says she wants the government to tackle the issue of prevention after that."

The segment cut to Tara Gomes, a drug policy research scientist at St. Michael's Hospital.

A tsunami hit me. Roger was dead. It was reported on The National; it must be true. That broadcast penetrated a thin membrane in my brain that had been my last protection. "... He was found dead in a parking lot in downtown Toronto from a fentanyl overdose."

Roger's name scrolled across the bottom of the TV screen. I collapsed to the floor, broken.

Calling All Angels

The snow came early in December as I sank further into grief. Christmas lights replaced pumpkins, and I struggled to find joy. Shut in and shattered, I forensically read every text, message, and email from Roger and every reply I had made. I was searching for what lay hidden between the lines. What had I missed? Why did I not see his relapse coming?

My one reprieve was on Sundays when Lucy unfailingly picked me up for church. It was Advent, and we prepared to celebrate the birth of Jesus. After Mass, we sat over cappuccinos and Pastel de Nata at Caldense Bakery and reminisced about past Christmases.

Last year, Lucy had hosted a festive arts-and-crafts night at her home. We had made Christmas-candle centrepieces from the birch saplings she had harvested at the cottage. It had been a grand night with friends as we drank wine, ate, then transformed the little logs into centrepieces using glue guns and glitter, festive ribbons, holly, and Christmas baubles.

"What will we do this year, Lucy?"

"Linda told me about shoeboxes for charity. We could do that," she suggested. "We could fill shoeboxes with Christmas toiletries and treats for those in need."

"That's a good idea," I perked up. "What about Alpha House? We could make shoeboxes for the guys and give them some cheer for the holidays."

So began Roger's 1st Memorial Christmas Shoeboxes for Alpha House. The home and lads there had given so much to Roger in his recovery. They were his Ohana.

Lucy and I set the date, and I emailed my closest contacts. It read:

> Calling all Angels,
>
> I'm having a Christmas Craft night on Friday, December

15, with Lucy and the girls.

We're making Christmas Shoeboxes, decorating and filling them for the guys at Alpha House (where Roger lived in recovery). Let's put a surprise box of treats under the Christmas tree for them.

We estimate a cost of $20/box. Lucy is donating the shoeboxes, and we'll provide everything else. A Lasagne dinner too! Can you come, 6pm, please?

If you can't make it, will you consider a donation, $20 to fill a box?

Love,

Irene

Soon my inbox pinged with RSVPs and offers of donations. In no time, we had reached our goal with enough contributions to fill twenty boxes. When we started the project, I could not have known how it would lift my spirits. My brain switched to focus on the details. I prepared a spreadsheet of donors and RSVPs, the menu, and the shopping list. The adrenalin that had fuelled my fear now sparked a neuron of hope.

Lucy and I brainstormed about what to include in the boxes and created a Santa List:

Slippers, socks, shampoo, toothbrush and toothpaste, a mug, hot chocolate, cookies, chocolates, notebook, pen, Christmas cracker, and a special card. Thanks to the generosity of friends, we also had enough to include a ten-dollar gift certificate for A&W in each box.

I chose A&W because a new location had recently opened near Alpha House. Roger's eyes always lit up whenever I gave him a gift card, and A&W was his favourite. I smiled to think of the boys walking over for a Teen Burger or a Chubby Chicken. It meant more than the monetary value; it was about the camaraderie of friends sharing a moment in a bright new restaurant.

We went on a shopping spree with our list in hand. First to the Dollar Store for Christmas paper and tissue to wrap and line the twenty boxes, then we worked through the list. We had two carts full. I apologized to the unlucky shopper behind us in the queue, as the cashier diligently scanned each item.

We were on a mission. Next, we drove to IKEA. Happy and hungry, we headed straight to the cafeteria for the signature Swedish meatballs with mashed potatoes and lingonberry jam; even my taste buds were waking up. We set out through the store, obediently following the arrows on the floor. Although a Kivic sofa or a Tarva bed frame wasn't on the list, we still had fun window shopping as we wandered on our way to the kitchen wares. There, we found inexpensive Vardera mugs in a selection of colours.

"These are perfect, Lucy! What do you think? Blue or green?"

"Let's get ten of each," she said.

In the Market Hall area, resplendent in Christmas decorations, we ooh-ed and aah-ed. Festive bits and bobs found their way into our cart. That one trip to IKEA with Lucy did more for my mental wellbeing than months of antidepressants. By the time we rolled up to the Christmas tree shop in the outside parking lot, I wanted to buy one. The light was fading as we jostled for just the right tree—not too big, not too small. The cold air was heady with the scent of pine, as we crunched the bed of needles shaken from their branches underfoot.

At twenty dollars each, the trees were flying off the lot. We settled on the perfect size for me. It stood inches above my head, just over five-feet tall. We paid up and bundled it into Lucy's SUV with our other wares and headed back to my place. The pointed tree poked between our heads, and the mugs chimed together over each bump in the road. I looked in the rear-view mirror and shivered. The year before, Roger had been with us, wedged in the back with the Christmas tree. The biggest treasure of all was the hope we felt then. He had completed detox and was home for a few days before entering rehab at Renascent.

Back home, my days were full of plans to make the Alpha House Shoe Box night a success. I had wanted to turn the lights out on Christmas; now, I was putting up a tree and decorating it for the gathering. I climbed into my storeroom and pulled out Rubbermaid tubs full of Christmas decorations and ornaments collected since the boys were babies. I unwrapped them one by one: the keepsake teddy bear from Roger's first Christmas in 1988, the traced hands made into angel wings the boys had made at school, the Hawaiian Santa dressed in shorts and Aloha shirt playing the ukulele, on and on. Each treasure connected me to memories of Roger and Brandon. I cried as I hooked and hung them. This was my first Christmas alone. Brandon was back in Europe with his girlfriend. Lighting the tree had always been about my boys, seeing them smile. I switched on the lights and a rainbow of colours blurred through the lens of my tears.

I prepared for the Christmas craft night. My fingers were raw with paper cuts from folding and assembling the twenty cardboard boxes and lids. I piled them high in the corner by the dining table. The supplies were still strewn across my bedroom floor. I needed to organize an area in the living room to display them in easy reach for my friends, the Christmas elves. In my storage room, there was an old wicker unit with four shelves, and I resolved to haul it out the next day. I cake-walked my way through the room and crawled into bed.

I woke with purpose and checked my to-do list for December 6. My calendar had a star to remind me it was the annual Les Clefs d'Or Christmas party. Julie had invited me as her plus-one. I had RSVP'd yes, even though I was unsure of stepping out. I looked in my closet and picked out a little sequined black dress and thought of the old me who once wore it.

My first task of the day was to bring the shelving unit out of the storage room. But before I could move it, I had to empty it. In the tight space, I reached for the first box and slid it towards me and saw "Roger" scrolled across the cardboard in black sharpie ink. My hand recoiled as if I had touched an electric burner. My instinct was to run out of the room, slam and lock the door. But I stood frozen in the tight space. Roger's personal effects were at my fingertips. After he passed, in all the confusion and pain, Jen had taped them up in boxes and stored them away. "You can sort them out when you're ready, Irene," she had said.

"Dear God, give me strength," I breathed and reached for the box again.

One by one, I brought the boxes into the light and space of the living room. Christmas carols played on the radio as I made a cup of Earl Grey tea to steady myself. Holding the steaming mug, I sat cross-legged in the middle of Roger's rug with four boxes and a big bag surrounding me. The Christmas tree towered in the corner with mocking merriment. I inhaled and reached for the nearest box. Tearing the tape off the top was like ripping a Band-Aid off my heart.

A stranger, looking at the contents, would see in it the things Roger treasured, a picture of a young man fighting for life against the disease of addiction.

An accordion file held the inspirational cards I'd sent him. I fingered the envelopes and traced the words of hope inside. "You can do it, Roger!" "You Got This!" A Christmas card signed, "This Moment is Full of Love, Merry Christmas, Mum xxx." He had kept the cards through bouts of homelessness and relapse.

His Certificates of Completion from recent programs at Renascent, Oasis, and Alpha House were filed with care. There was a treasured picture of us together as a family and a framed photo inscribed, "I cannot change yesterday. I can only make the most of today and look with hope towards tomorrow."

Another box held his books, including the royal-blue Narcotics Anonymous hardback with the small pocketbook edition. Inscribed inside the jacket, a message said, "To my friend Roger. Jim B."

His leather-covered AA Big Book was dog-eared and highlighted. Mike, Roger's counsellor, had given him the cover for his birthday during his first year of rehab. Roger's one-year sobriety medallion was inside the compartment in the front. A spiral binder held worksheets from the Oasis program. He had completed a new resume, and detailed plans for his future goals. Goal number-one read:

"To make my family proud."

Roger's recovery journal listed his fears and hopes. He had kept a volume of *The Great Gatsby* from his recent adult education course. Nestled beside it was *On the Night You Were Born*, a little hardback book by Nancy Tillman. Inside, I had written, ".... The Moon Smiled. I loved you from that moment to forever! Mum xxx." I flipped through the pages: "... So whenever you doubt just how special you are and you wonder who loves you, how much and how far, listen for the geese honking high in the sky. They're singing a song to remember you by."

I had scrolled in a gold metallic pen across the bottom of this page: "Roger, we Love you."

Now, the knot in my stomach leapt to strangle my throat as I saw the box labelled "CLOTHES." I was on all fours, hyperventilating, with Roger's life and dreams scattered on our carpet. I crawled over the books to the bathroom where I wretched and choked for air. My head heaved over the toilet bowl as I hunched on my knees, both hands hugging the cold porcelain.

My phone pinged in the distance, twice. Some cosmic SOS rang out over the ether. I drew myself to the sound as I gagged on vomit. Then the phone rang. I fumbled to grab it and saw two texts had popped up.

"Thinking of you." From Kathy.

"Are you okay?" Jenifer asked.

Then Jen's face lit up the caller ID. I answered on the last ring.

"H, H, Hi." I hiccupped, sucking in air so I wouldn't pass out.

"Irene … Are you okay? I felt you heavy in my heart."

"I'm, I'm…."

"Breathe, Irene."

"How … how did you know?"

"I felt a heaviness in my chest, and something made me call you."

"Roger … his stuff … the boxes … he's gone."

"I know, Irene. … Breathe. It's okay. I'm here. I'll stay with you."

I snorted and blew my nose.

"Can you put the kettle on?" she said.

Jen talked me through until I caught my breath, until I made a cup of tea, until I could talk. We were both on speakerphone. She was driving to the Tampa airport from her home in Port Charlotte to catch a flight to Hawaii.

"I'm sorry, Jen." I gasped.

The hot, sweet tea flushed the burning acid down my throat. She talked, and I listened until I could lift my head. I told her how I had pulled out Roger's boxes. She had taped them up and stored them away on the old wicker shelf. She had said, "When you're ready Irene, you can sort them out." I could never be ready, but Pandora's box was open now.

"Okay, Irene … sort through what to keep, and what you can let go of."

With her voice to console me, I filled a black garbage bag with Roger's old surfer and skateboarding magazines for recycling. The chaos in my head subsided, and my breath returned to a slower rhythm.

"You're gonna be okay, Irene. I have to go." She was pulling into the airport parking lot.

"Bye, Jen. It's a miracle you called."

"I'll call you tomorrow. I love you."

I reread the two texts from my friends and felt God's hands on the wheel of this intervention. My friends were angels on this earth. I fed on Jen's strength and continued to sort through Roger's folders. I tossed old papers and appointment reminders, fighting hard not to read each date and with whom.

To the side was a small acrylic keepsake box. Inside it was the jade stone wrapped in silver wire and strung on a cord. I had given it to Roger on his twenty-sixth birthday. As I held it in my palm, the energy transported me to that day at the crystal store on Queen Street West. I had picked out the oddly shaped green stone for its spiritual properties of health and harmony, and now it was back in my hands. A stepping-stone. A wee voice in my head said, *"You got this, Mum."*

The room grew dim in the early dusk, and I struggled to my feet. Christmas carols were playing on CHFI radio. I pulled my coat over my pyjamas, stuffed my feet into my boots, and wheeled my trolley across the parking lot to the recycling depot of my building. It was another step in letting go. Roger was in my heart, not in these things. I stepped back from the bin a bit lighter.

Returning to my apartment, I saw the black dress hanging on the back of the bedroom door and checked the big clock; it was 4:30 p.m. Julie was due to pick me up at 5:15. If I hurried, I could go to the party. It was the last thing I wanted to do, but what was the alternative? I fixed a bowl of cornflakes and took a bath, dunking my head under the water to wash away the pain and sickness from every pore and strand of hair. Stepping out of the bath, I shed the broken shell of myself. I blow-dried my thin hair, rolling it up out of my peely-wally face. I moisturized and brushed on a layer of foundation, dabbing around my swollen eyes. I lined my lips and applied lipstick, swiped gold eye shadow over my puffed eyelids, and followed with a few swipes of black mascara. I squinted at the mirror. With my glasses off, I was half blind and didn't look half bad. I prayed the lighting would be dim at the party.

The shimmery dress fit loosely, but I wore my vintage Goodwill cashmere cardigan over the top. It was a pale peach colour with a cream fur stole attached. Black stockings and high-heeled shoes completed my outfit—almost. I reached for Roger's jade talisman, Health and Harmony. I slipped it in my satin evening bag and hurried out the door.

Julie and I stepped into the warmth of a festive ballroom at the top of the Thompson Hotel, adorned with glitz and full of glamorous people. The CN Tower filled the full picture window, illuminated in candy-cane green and red. It was no match for the silver glow of the full moon that hung from heaven by its side, a haloed light with a shadow of a smile. Someone handed me a glass of champagne.

"You got this, Mum!"

We Grieve Thousands

December 11, 2017

I woke. In the gloomy winter light, the clock on my night table blinked 11 a.m. I shifted down under the duvet to sleep and let go, trying to reassure myself I was too late.

The night before, I had read a call-to-action on the Toronto Overdose Prevention Site:

> "Join us. March. Monday, December 11 at Moss Park—meet at 12 noon. We Grieve Thousands, a mournful action in honour of the thousands we have lost to government inaction."

The post discussion informed participants to dress warmly, wear black, and bring a picture of their loved one.

It was a blood-freezing, grey morning: -8°C. I shuffled to the bathroom and splashed my face with water. How I wanted to go back to bed and shut the world out. Over my pyjamas, I layered jeans, sweaters, two pairs of socks, black boots, a long black scarf wrapped twice around my neck, and a winter hat. Over the top, I wore my ankle-length black down coat. I grabbed Roger's framed photo and put it in my backpack. No breakfast for me, just a scoop of dry food for Mr. Kitty, and out the door.

A bus ride and two subway transfers later, I emerged at the intersection of Queen and Yonge Streets. It was already noon as I hustled, head bent against the sharp wind, east towards Moss Park. The rally, over a hundred strong, had gathered and now surged towards me onto Queen Street. They waved placards: "THEY TALK/ WE DIE." and some waved cutouts of black coffins marked with names of loved ones. The front line held up a white banner stretched the width of the road. "WE GRIEVE THOUSANDS." was scrolled across it in huge black capital letters, with a body outline splattered in red ink. I turned around and found myself in-step behind the banner. The crowd chanted behind me.

"They talk. We die!"

I fumbled to get Roger's picture out of my backpack and held it up.

I looked over and saw the corner parking lot at Jarvis Street where Roger's body had been found.

"We die!" The crowd chanted.

I lowered my head and made the sign of the cross for Roger and for all of us.

To my left, a young protester struggled to hold up his side of the banner against the icy wind. He was grappling with a large black grocery bag that slipped from his arms.

"Let me carry that for you," I offered.

He passed it to me, and I slung it over my shoulder. It was awkward, but not too heavy. I kept in step, not knowing where we were going, and joined in the chanting. A CP24 News cameraman walked backwards in front of us to catch the action. I hoped he wouldn't fall on the ice.

At Church Street, two mounted police on black stallions joined the front of the march. The horse's hides shone in the cold sunshine; steam blew from their nostrils. The traffic was stopped as we surged forward towards Queen and Yonge Streets—one of the busiest intersections in Toronto. Here we ran into teams of red-clad Toronto soccer fans lined up to cheer the Toronto FC soccer team's victory parade. The team had won the hard-fought Major League Soccer championship trophy—the first Canadian team to win the cup in the history of the Major League Soccer.

As we approached the packed Nathan Phillips Square, Mayor John Tory was giving a speech proclaiming December 11 as "Red Day" in honour of Toronto FC. It was bedlam, and the police blocked our entrance. Instead, we marched up the side of Bay Street and merged with the sea of red supporters as we snaked our way to City Hall. We walked one by one through the heavy wooden doors, dropping the placards outside. I was still carrying the shopping bag, and the boy who had walked beside me took it from my shoulder. It held a megaphone.

Assembled now in the rotunda, the megaphone passed from speaker to speaker, each one's grief amplified as they spoke of the loved ones they'd lost. Some told of their own struggles with the lack of harm-reduction services. The anguish and pain set against the cheering fans outside was jarring.

Zoe Dodd, a harm-reduction worker and activist, took the megaphone and called out the Mayor and politicians for the city's inaction to the opioid crisis and the police for their insensitivity.

"We are fighting for our fucking lives here! You talk! We die!"

Her cry echoed up the circular rotunda where civil servants, emerging from their glass cubicles, ringed the gallery. We lay on the marble floor strewn with red roses—a die-in. A litany of loved ones' names was called out as a banner dropped from above. It reached from the second floor to the ground, emblazoned with:

"WE GRIEVE THOUSANDS!"

Security and police presence gathered around the periphery, keeping watch. Their mission was to protect the peace, but any peace in our hearts had shattered.

I lay motionless on the floor, holding onto Roger's picture frame with the prayer still taped to the back of it. It had been there since the Recovery Day rally. If ever a prayer was needed, it was now. I made my way in a slow crawl to Zoe and asked her quietly if I could say a prayer. Soon, the megaphone was in one of my trembling hands. I held up Roger's photo in the other.

"This is my son Roger," my voice rose. "He died walking-distance from this spot. Across from Moss Park before they opened the supervised injection site. We need harm reduction. I remember him and all our loved ones."

I had to shift my gait to stop myself from keeling over. The megaphone shook in my hand. My teeth chattered and my body shivered.

"We remember them. In the rising of the sun and in its going down, we remember them."

The refrain echoed back louder and louder with each lament.

> "In the blowing of the wind and in the chill of winter, we remember them. In the opening of buds and in the rebirth of spring, we remember them. In the blueness of the sky and in the warmth of summer, we remember them. In the rustling of leaves and in the

beauty of autumn, we remember them. At the beginning of the year and when it ends, we remember them. When we are weary and in need of strength, we remember them. When we are lost and sick at heart, we remember them. When we have joys we yearn to share, we remember them. So long as we live, they too shall live, for they are now a part of us, as we remember them."

"We remember them." The chant rose to the ceiling.

I finished in tears and handed the megaphone back to Zoe.

A young man came over to me, sobbing. He hugged me tight. What was his story? Who had he lost? This collective grief engulfed my pain. I wanted to offer solace, but the prayer was all I had. I was about to stagger away when a woman came up to me.

"You're his mum!" she said.

I was still holding the photo; she had recognized Roger.

"I was working at the Fred Victor ... the centre ... the morning they found your son. I was called out because they thought it might be one of our clients. I went to him."

My body sank as if underwater. I couldn't reach the surface. Her words came to me as if through an echo chamber while the rally blurred around me. This angel of a woman dressed in a beige puffy coat held me in a tight hug. She had knelt by my Roger's body. She had stayed with him until the coroner arrived. It had haunted her.

"I wondered who his family was ... he had no ID on him," her words floated towards me.

"Did he look like he was sleeping?" I asked.

"Yes, he looked peaceful."

I held onto her and her words. God had put her there. He had dragged me out of bed that morning for our paths to cross. I wanted to ask more questions, but I was shutting down. I had to go before I collapsed. I saw a coffee shop near the exit and swam towards it. An old man approached me.

"What's all this about?" he asked.

"It's the opioid crisis. People are dying," I cried.

"How can I help? What can I do?"

"It can be anyone's child." I showed him Roger's photo.

Turning away, I saw a group of policemen on alert. Some choice words had been yelled about police insensitivity. Something made me stop and speak to the officers.

"I know you have a hard job, but I beg you, if you attend to a body lying on the street, please treat it with dignity and remember me, a mum suffering. Everyone is somebody's someone. You look like family men. You would want that for your own child."

Their shoulders slumped and their faces softened. I saw tears in their eyes, or maybe they reflected the tears in mine.

The Assembly Line

December 2017

I floundered in the days leading up to the Christmas Box assembly. The gifts for Alpha House lay like hostages in their shopping bags on my bedroom floor. The living room carpet was a minefield of Roger's belongings I avoided as I traversed from my bed to the kitchen and back. My abandoned to-do list read: Remove shelving from storage.

The antidepressants had layered a thin gauze over my heart. Now it bled as the gauze was ripped off. Before I could pull out the shelves, I needed to clear the living room. As I reached for the box labelled "CLOTHES", I jumped back as if I'd touched a fire. Inside lay the clothes Roger was wearing when they found him.

"Breathe, just breathe," I heard Jen's voice in my mind.

I buried my head in Roger's jacket. In his pocket I found two business cards for social workers he would never see again. I was in a daze, battling to stave off another breakdown.

"Breathe, just breathe."

Frantically, I folded the clothes and sorted the books, photos, and files. I stuffed them into the big Rubbermaid tub that had held the Christmas decorations. The lid snapped into place as I collapsed my weight across it.

"Don't stop! Keep going." I was talking to myself.

I mustered the strength to drag the wicker-shelving unit into the living room.

My knees buckled as I pushed the container into the storage closet where the shelves had been. Slamming the door shut, I leaned against it and slid to the floor.

My stomach growled, reminding me I was still alive. In my fridge, the nearly empty shelves held a carton with two eggs. I boiled them, peeled off the steaming shells, and chopped them into a salad with a squirt of mayonnaise and dash of salt. I found some stale crackers. Mr. Kitty's hopes rose when he saw me eating and he snuggled beside me. On a good day, I would open a can of soft cat food for him—he hoped this might be one of them.

A watery sunlight filtered through the icy windows. The trees, stripped of their finery, waved skeletal arms against the wind. The birds had long taken refuge. The afternoon GO Train screeched on the nearby tracks towards the junction. Life sped past outside as I watched from my fourth-floor concrete box.

Switching on the Christmas-tree lights, I raised the volume on the radio to drown out my thoughts. I mustered the energy to go into the bedroom and brought the bags of supplies to stock the shelves. The top shelf held all twenty pairs of men's slippers; toiletries, notebooks, and pens lined the middle shelf; and, the mugs stuffed with hot chocolate, Christmas crackers and treats filled the bottom. I looped garlands around the frame. The crowning glory was a Hawaiian woodcut red "Mele Kalikimaka" sign I had brought all the way from the Big Island. I hung it from the top. Roger would like that.

I organised the workstation for the assembly line; the dining table would be the cutting and wrapping station. I brought in the patio table and spruced it up with a cheap red tablecloth; this would be the filling station. I set up a smaller table for card writing.

"It's beginning to look a lot like Christmas," sang out from the radio.

There was no going back now. My friend Landy had made a generous donation to cover the cost of the food and beverages. I trooped to Loblaws with a grocery list for lasagne, salad, focaccia, dessert, and wine.

"In for a penny, in for a pound," I heard my mum's words in my head as I reached for the cheese and olives.

The big night arrived with an arctic blast and a dusting of light snow. The trees outside had snatched a shimmer of snowflakes to dress for the party. I fluffed pillows, arranged glasses, and lit candles. Mmm … a blast of cheesy lasagne filled the kitchen when I opened the oven. My cheeks turned red, and for once, it wasn't from crying. Warmth radiated through my apartment. I was in my full-on butler mode.

I changed into a white t-shirt with "Ho, Ho, Ho" in green and red letters across the front and a red skirt just as the buzzer rang. Lucy and Linda arrived first, bowling me over with hugs and kisses and coats. The buzzer rang again and again. My coat closet overflowed with parkas, and snow boots lined the hallway. My friends brought wine, appetizers, laughter, and love.

"Hello, welcome! Make yourself at home."

I didn't have to repeat myself. The girls crushed into the living room, happy to see old friends. The elves had clocked in to work and to play.

"Great to see you! Look at this place! It's like Santa's workshop!" Jill went straight to the shelves to check out all the Christmas treats ready for the boxes. I ladled glasses full of hot mulled wine. The heady aroma of cinnamon, cloves, and oranges mixed with the smell of bread and lasagne warming in the oven.

"Ahh," I exhaled in the kitchen, Lucy by my side. She looked radiant in a red velvet top and flowing skirt, her brown hair falling in waves to her shoulders.

"Thank you, Lucy," I said.

God knows there would have been no tree, no treats, and no boxes without her.

"Come on, Irene! Let's get started. Everything looks great," she hugged me.

Linda set up a demonstration by the dining table to show us how to transform the plain shoeboxes into festive containers. First, she measured and cut the paper to fit the bottom and the lid. Then she folded the colourful wrapping paper over the box, taping it in place. I had the honour of filling up the first one.

"Voila!" I held the box up like Mufasa holding Simba. We raised our glasses. "Cheers! Only nineteen more to go," we laughed.

I popped on the lid and tied it up with tinsel; it was so much more than the contents—it was a Christmas box full of love and aloha.

Before the assembly line rolled into action, we ate, then got to work. Lucy and Linda held court with Mary, measuring, cutting, and wrapping.

"Who has nice handwriting?" I asked.

Nancy showed me her cursive penmanship.

"You're on for the Christmas cards."

Thrilled to have a sit-down job, she began writing a personal note with a flourish on every card.

Amy and Kyomi teamed up to mark $10 on the A&W cards and place them in their gift envelopes. Jill, Sandra, and Jocelyne filled the boxes while Rosalie, with her penchant for quality control, checked the contents against the list before the lid went on.

For my part, I flitted around like a festive foreman, giving encouraging words, dispensing wine, and snapping pictures. It was magic. Soon the shelves were empty and the floor was littered with scraps of wrapping paper.

"All done!" We cheered as the last lid went on.

We piled the boxes in a pyramid on the dining table—they stacked higher than our heads. Click. We took a selfie. Even before we delivered the boxes to Alpha House, I had received the best gift of all: the Christmas spirit.

A Tale of Two Tables

December 24, 2017

"The Best French Christmas Eve Dinner in Toronto," the invitation promised. I arrived at my friend Xavier's home during the tail-end of a blizzard. My boots crunched the frost as I walked up the driveway. Wind swept the snow from the roof, swirling it around me as if in a snow globe, the fluffy flakes catching on my eyelashes and nose. I hesitated at the front door, taking it all in—the Christmas lights, laughter, and music escaping through the windows. I fought to match my mood to the merriment. It was my first Christmas alone, without Roger and Brandon.

"Fake it till you make it." Those cliché words of wisdom echoed in my head.

The door opened. I kicked off my boots and shed my winter coat, shaking the snow from my hair.

"Welcome! Merry Christmas!" A chorus of friends greeted me.

My anxiety slowly melted with the warmth of their hugs. Children played by the Christmas tree, their excitement escaping like the bubbles from the popped champagne bottles. Someone handed me a glass.

"Cheers!"

The fizz tickled my throat, and I lost myself in chatter and cheer.

A festive buffet overflowed with the finest hors d'oevres: canapés, foie gras, and smoked salmon. The aroma of roasted turkey wafted from the kitchen, where Aviva was busy putting final touches on Christmas dinner. A feast for all the senses was served course by course with accompanying wines. By the time the macarons were served, I looked at my watch Cinderella-style. It was 11 p.m.—I planned to attend Midnight Mass at St. Michael's Cathedral—it was a tradition with my boys, and I wanted to carry it on this year. So far, I'd held my emotions intact without shattering on this first Christmas since Roger's death. Fortunately, another family was leaving at the same time and offered to drive me downtown.

A luminous blanket of snow covered the city. What a difference from the last time I walked this same path to St. Michaels through St. James's Park with Roger. It had been last Easter Sunday. He was three months into recovery then, so alive and aware of where he was and where he'd been. He commented on the park benches where homeless people were gathered.

"I've slept there, Mum, but I'm walking in the light now," he had said.

"That's right, son, in the light now."

The cathedral had been packed; Roger and I had found a spot behind the back pew. Cardinal Collins gave a sermon on light and darkness, and I felt he was speaking directly to us.

"We walk in the light of the risen Jesus."

Later, when he proceeded down the centre aisle to administer the Easter blessing, he turned and walked past where we stood. His embroidered ivory robes brushed against us as he sprinkled the holy water on our heads. I held Roger's hand and joy flowed through me as the boys' choir sang out, "Hallelujah."

We'd been among the first to follow the procession out of the cathedral into the courtyard. Roger walked over to the Archbishop and shook his hand—a snapshot I hold in my heart. Roger wasn't shy. He was, after all, "Roger the Famous", his childhood nickname. As a boy growing up in Hawaii, he had been full of confidence and aloha spirit.

Now, I walked alone through the snow to midnight Christmas Mass. The red neon sign of Fran's Diner pulsed in the dark. With half an hour to spare and feeling light-headed from the champagne, I stopped in for a hot drink. My cheeks flushed as the warmth hit my face. I looked around the restaurant and saw a motley crew scattered throughout the booths and Formica® tables. The harsh lights were sobering. I sat by the bar and ordered a coffee. Three well-dressed men sat nearby at a high-top table—wise men maybe not, but certainly wisecracking.

"Hi, Little Red Riding Hood," they scoffed at my red beret.

I smiled as the church bells started to chime. It was time to go. Bolstered by the caffeine, I trudged the short distance through the snow. I wasn't late, but as I walked down the aisle of the cathedral, I saw that all the seats were taken. I reached the altar and knelt to admire the Nativity scene. As I turned to walk to the standing-room-only crowd at the back, a couple shifted in their pew and beckoned me to sit down. Glory be to God! I had a front-row seat; there was room at the inn.

The organ pipes bellowed and the St. Michael's Boys Choir raised their voices to the ceiling with "Joy to the World". The sound echoed through every crack in my heart. As Christmas Eve turned to Christmas Day, I was with God and He was with me.

When Mass ended, the Archbishop raised his hands in blessing, "The peace of the Lord be always with you."

I turned to my neighbours, tears of gratitude in my eyes. "And peace be with you," I said.

I was one of the last to leave the cathedral. Surprised that the Archbishop was still in the cold courtyard, I walked over, bowed, and shook his hand. I looked up at the frosty heavens and whispered, *"This is for you, Roger."*

I rushed to catch the subway but missed the last bus from Royal York. The snow insulated the night as I walked up the deserted road home. Christmas lights draped the trees and twinkled in the windows. My anxiety at facing this first Christmas alone lifted; I felt suspended between the past and the future. I was in the now.

I woke up late on Christmas morning with Mr. Kitty meowing loudly to remind me it was past his breakfast time. While waiting for coffee to brew, I took an inventory of the cupboards. There was a ten-pound bag of potatoes, eyes winking at me. What had I been thinking when I bought them weeks ago?

"Only ninety-nine cents," the cashier had said. Sold! Well, after all I'm Scottish—potatoes and penny-pinching are in my DNA. Now here they were, threatening to put down roots in my kitchen.

I opened the fridge and found a family-size pack of ground beef—a gift from Sandra, and me with no family to cook for—also carrots, celery, onions, tomatoes, and mushrooms. Clearly, I had the ingredients for shepherd's pie, and it dawned on me where I could serve it. I set to work, braising the beef, sautéing the vegetables, boiling and mashing the potatoes. I cranked up the volume to my favourite Christmas soundtrack, *Love Actually*. My jaw dropped as the Beach Boys sang out, "If you should ever leave me…"

As I stirred and seasoned, my tears entered the recipe.

It was afternoon by the time I spread a thick, creamy layer of mashed potatoes over the mince casserole and put it in the oven. When it was done, I turned the heat down and popped in two loaves of crusty bread. The aroma comforted me.

I took the shepherd's pie out of the oven; it was perfect for a big Christmas dinner. I looked over at the empty dining table and shuddered. I wrapped foil around the pie dish and swaddled it in a bath towel to keep the heat in. In a large carrying bag, I packed paper plates, plastic cutlery, and napkins left over from Roger's memorial tea. I quickly changed out of my pyjamas; it was already getting dark when I called a cab. I planned to visit my girlfriend later, so I donned my good red coat and beret—it was Christmas Day, after all. I slung the bags over my shoulder and cradled the hot shepherd's pie in my arms like a baby. I was a contortionist, balancing it on my knee as I tried to lock the door. I laughed at my antics in the elevator, almost dropping it as I reached for the lobby button.

The taxi was already at the curb when I walked out into the cold late afternoon. I motioned to the driver for help, and he came round and opened the car door.

"Where to?"

"Moss Park," I said.

"The park?" he asked. I caught his raised eye in the rearview mirror.

It was not a typical Christmas-party address.

"Yes, near the armoury," I said and settled into the back seat with the precious warm cargo on my lap.

The city flashed past as we sped eastbound on the Gardiner Expressway. The driver took the Jarvis Street exit. Looking out, I was shaken from my trance. We were stopped at traffic lights at the corner of Queen and Jarvis. To my left was the parking lot where Roger died. Panic engulfed me. For the umpteenth time, I asked myself the impossible question of *"Why? Why did Roger have to die?"* An eternity passed before the lights changed—long enough for Roger's twenty-eight years of life to unfold in my heart.

Across the street, a light shone from the trailer of the Moss Park Overdose Prevention Site. This beacon of hope for somebody's son or daughter had opened only weeks after Roger overdosed. If only it had been operating the night my son had relapsed, the night one last needle of fentanyl-laced heroin killed him.

Soon, the taxi pulled to a stop, and the driver came around and opened the door. He held my bundled shepherd's pie as I stepped into a slushy snowbank. I steadied myself and blinked away my tears.

"Are you okay?" he asked.

"Yes," I said, but God knows I wasn't.

I approached the trailer slowly. Someone had set up a banquet table in the snow in front of an open tent. The table was full of donated food: pizzas, sandwiches, and even a crock-pot. Two girls, somebody's daughters, were sitting in the cold tent, smoking. A young man approached me. He offered to clear a space on the table for my offering. I sat the pie down on a chair to unwrap it. When I turned, he had disappeared, and no space had been cleared. I told the girls about the plates and utensils in the bag and made a spot for the shepherd's pie. They barely looked up. I felt conspicuously dressed in my bright red coat with a Swarovski crystal snowflake pinned on my lapel. I wished I was invisible. What right did I have to encroach on this cold Christmas buffet? I may have looked privileged, but the only privilege I had was giving my boy life. To share his journey, even down the dark path of addiction, through recovery, and sudden death.

This was not a Hallmark Christmas movie. Not everyone lived happily ever after. Not everyone got to live. But there were angels—the frontline volunteers who worked in the trenches of harm reduction, prepared to administer the life-saving dose of Naloxone to reverse the effects of an opioid overdose.

I stumbled to the nearby 501 streetcar stop at Queen and Jarvis. I struggled to stand. I saw the snow-covered parking lot across the street, and for a moment I reassured myself that Roger's body hadn't frozen that summer night, lying in the shadows until sunrise. It was small consolation, but I was grasping for a needle of light in the abyss of darkness. I drew in a sharp breath.

God only knows what I am without you, Roger.

People Die All the Time

January 2018

"You're late, Irene," the receptionist said when I checked in for my doctor's appointment. I swallowed hard and tugged to unravel the scarf wrapped twice around my neck. It was bitter out, and my glasses fogged up in the heat of the reception area.

"I'm sorry, but …" How could I be late? I'd waited since before Christmas for this appointment. I had tattooed it in my brain along with my return-to-work date of January 7, 2018.

"Take a seat. I'll see if the doctor can squeeze you in," she smiled.

The waiting room was full of patients seated on grey chairs lined up in rows facing the white door. Periodically, a nurse would pop her head out and call for the next patient. Windows looked onto Bay Street where a sleety snow fell. I removed my winter boots and placed them on the mat under the black sign that read, "Remove Your Shoes." My socks soaked up the salty puddle on the floor. I hopped to an empty seat and waited. My heart thumped in panic as I pulled off my coat and hat. I thought I was early for an 11 a.m. appointment, only to be told I'd missed my 10 a.m. slot.

In my backpack, I could feel the folder holding the papers I had received from the insurance company. They deemed my breakdown a short-term disability. Was there an expiry date on grief? Some algorithm had plotted the return-to-work date, and here I was at the doctor's with a fistful of forms for a means test.

"Irene?" The nurse's head popped through the door. Her black hair toppled over her glasses as she scanned the waiting area for me.

"Here!" I felt like a child being called into the principal's office.

She walked me down a hallway past a warren of rooms and parked me in an empty examination room. There was always the false sense of expectation at this point. *"Oh, it's my turn,"* you think. In fact, it was merely phase two of the wait. I sat in the familiar grey room on the chair squeezed between the sink and the desk and stared at the wall in front of me. I squinted to test my eyesight on the eye exam poster.

Then I noticed a glint on the wall, a disk of light. It moved up and down, up and down. Mesmerized, I felt the beat of my heart in the rhythm. I looked down and saw the silver medallion I wore with Roger's picture inside. It rested on my chest. I placed my hand on it, and the orb of light disappeared. I took my hand away, and it reflected my heartbeat: thump, thump. I felt Roger's presence in the room and meditated with deep breaths on the reflection as it slowed to a steady tick-tock. The room was still and cold. I felt Roger's message like Morse code on the wall: *"Don't worry, Mum."*

The door flew open and the doctor's presence shattered the silence. "You're late, Irene."

"I'm sorry. I know. I didn't mean to. I'm so confused." I sat to attention.

The doctor took her seat facing the computer on the desk. "What can I do for you today?"

My eyes filled with tears as I handed her the forms. "I can't go back to work tomorrow. I can't sleep. I can't concentrate."

"I don't have time for these forms today. Leave them with the secretary and make an appointment for next week. Are you taking the anti-depressants?"

"Yes." My voice quivered.

The printer rattled, and she reached down to pick up the paper. She handed me a new Pristiq prescription, increasing the dose from 50 mg to 100 mg. My hands shook, still clutching the insurance form.

"I'll see you next week, then." She left the room.

I gathered my backpack in one hand, the forms in the other with the prescription, and retraced my steps back to the reception, broken. The fluorescent lights in the foyer startled me as I tried to keep my composure. I handed the receptionist the papers.

"I have to come back next week."

"Same time, Irene. Don't be late."

The pharmacy was across from the reception, and I hurried over. In the short twenty steps, I had misplaced the prescription. I fumbled in my backpack.

"Take your time," the pharmacist smiled across the counter in his white jacket. I handed him my health card. "How are you?"

"It's been a hard day." I raised the white paper in surrender. "Here it is." The prescription answered his question.

"Take a seat. It will only take a few minutes."

I sank into the seat, bewildered, and tried to comprehend what had happened. My instinct told me to wean off the pills and let the fog lift. Yet, with a ten-minute consultation, the doctor had prescribed twice the dosage.

Back home, I put the box of pills out of sight in a drawer. I retreated to the sofa with my blanket and clutched Roger's medallion to my chest. I wanted to sleep and never wake up, but the nightmare shook me awake with a jerk.

A polar vortex settled over Toronto. The temperature dipped into negative double-digits, and I plunged further into despair. The Tuesday appointment loomed. I was so afraid of being late that I didn't sleep at all the night before. Return to work? That concierge desk was a cliff edge I couldn't throw myself over. I needed help.

From my visits to Women's College Hospital for mammograms and bone density tests, I remembered seeing a poster for a Women's Mental Health program. After a quick Google search, I downloaded a referral form. I packed it into my backpack with the never-opened box of Pristiq. A survival impulse surfaced in me as I showered and layered on clothes for the arctic morning commute.

I arrived at the doctor's office early. The waiting room was less hectic this time, and the nurse ushered me into the examination room. I sat with resolve, praying that the doctor would complete the insurance forms to extend my time off. There was no sunshine to glimmer on Roger's medallion. I twiddled it in my hand for strength.

The doctor breezed in a little less frazzled than she had been on my last visit. I was an early appointment, and the day hadn't caught up with her yet.

"Well now, Irene," she fingered the forms on her desk, "it's time to go back to work."

"I can't." I searched for words to explain the panic and turmoil inside of me. "I'm…" I shrunk into my shell. I knew I couldn't return to that desk where I'd sat for two long days when Roger went missing.

"Irene… people die all the time. Family, friends, relatives."

Her words pierced me like daggers.

"I know, but it's my son." My brain pounded. I wanted to yell, *"He's not people!"*

I had lost my sister and my mum in recent years. Those heartaches hurt, but for Roger, there wasn't a scale that could measure the pain. I crumpled.

The doctor submitted my referral to Women's College Hospital, and I left her to complete the insurance forms. I had shepherded Roger through recovery programs. Now I had advocated for my own recovery. I left the office in tears of resolve and walked across to the pharmacy.

The pharmacist recognized me and smiled. "How are you today?"

"A wee bit better than last week. Can you take these back?" I handed him the package of antidepressants.

It was time to face up to my pain and fears and not mask them.

I walked out onto Bay Street, a concrete canyon that blasted the brutal air up from Lake Ontario. My eyelashes and nose hairs froze. I crossed the intersection at Bay and Bloor, flanked on all corners by luxury flagship emporiums, their windows still dressed up with Christmas cheer.

Starbucks was a block away inside the Indigo bookstore. I rushed in before frost-bite nipped off my nose. I had a few hours before my afternoon appointment with Rosie, my Employee Assistance Program counsellor. I found a table at the edge of the café near the magazine section and claimed it by draping my coat over the chair. My anxiety settled as my toes thawed. I could breathe again. I rubbed my hands together to pump the blood to my fingertips and wrapped them around a tall cup of Verona roast coffee. The steam tickled my nose. This was better than any pill.

I sat down and took out my notepad and pencil. I wrote about what had just happened at the doctor's office, lest I forget. *"People die all the time."* I looked around, remembering how Roger and I loved to sit here together. He would get his skateboard magazines, and I would pick up *O* and *Vanity Fair* magazines. We would sit and read for hours. Although his seat beside me was empty, I sensed him there, and I felt warmth.

A girl sat facing me at the next table, her laptop between us. My eye caught a poem emblazoned on the back cover of her screen. I read it as tears spilled into my coffee. The poem was a sign from God directed at my heart. I scribbled the words into my notebook:

> Who will fix me now?
>
> Dive in when I'm down
>
> Save me from myself
>
> Don't let me drown.
>
> Who will make me fight?
>
> Drag me out alive
>
> Save me from myself
>
> Don't let me drown

Who Will Fix Me Now?

January – July 2018

Who will fix me now? The words wormed into my brain and the seed landed in a barren patch of hope. I had taken the first two steps to recovery: I admitted my grief was unmanageable, and I asked for help.

I counted the days until my appointment at the Women's College Hospital mental health department. Disability and mental health were unfamiliar to me; I'd spent my life supporting my family.

Brandon had returned to Europe. His girlfriend was studying in Estonia, and he joined her. His horizons were infinite, full of love and travel. At twenty-five, he was setting out in the world. He deserved his freedom. He had suffered silently the past seven years while I devoted my attention to Roger's recovery. Brandon, the quiet-natured younger brother, never complained.

"I'm good, Mum," he always said when asked, never wanting to add to my troubles.

"Mum, I'll stay if you want me to," Brandon had told me weeks after the funeral. And he would have.

"You go son, I'll be okay."

I couldn't bear the thought of my boy feeling responsible for me. That was my job. Lucy and I had driven him to the airport. I waved goodbye, mustering an enthusiasm that masked my heartbreak.

Now I lay alone, comatose, on the sofa with Mr. Kitty. I limped from day to day. I slept, wrote, and unravelled. I had enrolled in the Creative Writing program at the University of Toronto in 2015. Back then, my goal was to write a memoir titled, *It's Not the End of the World,* a collection of short stories of my adventures, travels, trials, and tribulations. Whatever the mishap—lost love, lost passport, lost roof over my head—I had a story and my best-friend Lorraine's sound advice: "It's not the end of the world, Irene."

But now, it was the end of my world, and the stories I had penned seemed trivial. Still, words kept coming. I wrote in my journal, my binder, on whatever scrap of paper I had at hand. My story of love, grief, and loss began to take shape. Writing was a lifeline that helped me manage the threads in my brain that had become a tangled mess. I cried words onto the page.

Spring exploded after the arctic winter melt. Ice floes breached the banks of the Humber River. My long-awaited appointment with Dr. Bruno arrived, and I ventured out of my apartment like a bear from hibernation. I had written the appointment time on my palm with a sharpie, terrified of being late. I entered Women's College Hospital through revolving doors and into the bright glass cube of the atrium. The fresh white marble floors were dotted with modern beige sofas—so different from the pine-scented infirmaries of my youth. I followed the path to the elevators, and I pushed the button for the seventh floor. I shuddered as it stopped with a bounce. The doors parted, and I spilled out into the reception area of the mental health unit.

The receptionist smiled as she checked my health card. "Take a seat. The doctor will call you."

The waiting room walls were bathed in a pale green hue with soft bucket seats arranged two-by-two around tables topped with leaflets affirming the hospital's vision and mission. I sat on the edge of a seat and waited and watched. A lady paraded nearby with a service animal, a hound dog with long velvety ears like the Hush Puppy in the shoe ads. She invited me to pet it. It looked at me with droopy bloodshot eyes and a wet nose and sat at my feet. I smiled. The knot in my stomach began to ease.

"Irene," I heard my name called.

I looked up to see a young woman in casual attire. She was tall with black wavy hair, a high forehead, and dark brows arched over kind brown eyes. She smiled and held out her hand.

"I'm Dr. Bruno, welcome."

I stood, fumbling to hold my bulky coat, and shook her hand. Her grip was firm. I followed her to her office.

"What brings you here, Irene?"

As I sat on the small sofa, I felt God had answered my silent plea: *Who will fix me now?*

Dr. Bruno gave me the space to speak and listened as I struggled to explain. She directed me with focused questions to determine the scale of my wellbeing. Her voice had a soft ring to it, not hurried, but precise.

"Are you eating, sleeping, and getting exercise? What medications are you taking?"

I explained I had stopped taking the antidepressants, and when she didn't object or reach for a prescription pad, I exhaled. The experience with my family doctor had scared me.

"The holidays are the hardest," I blurted out.

By then, I'd lived through one Hallowe'en birthday and Christmas without Roger.

I reached for my purple backpack and pulled out my spiral-bound journal. I opened it to "The Tale of Two Tables," a rough-draft story of how I had navigated Christmas. She took the journal and scanned the pages. My pencilled handwriting was more like hieroglyphs, with barely any grammar. I had sketched two oblong tables with the Christmas offerings scribbled on each. Tears stained the pages. Dr. Bruno's eyes lit up as she read and nodded. Her chair swivelled towards me, our knees inches apart. I shared my inner thoughts laid bare on the page—all the words I couldn't speak. They stuck in my throat but flowed from my pen. Me, a mum programmed to be a caregiver, began to trust this beautiful stranger to care for me.

"Irene, I hear you," she said.

My Road to Recovery

Spring – Summer 2018

"I'm coming, Roger! Where are you?" My voice cried out as the fog of sleep lifted.

I lay on sheets drenched with sweat, splintered between nightmares and delusion. Then the flush of adrenalin pulsed through my veins. My head throbbed. My maternal alarm system cranked into full gear before my brain sputtered to grasp reality.

"Why bother?" My thoughts sabotaged every effort I made to slide my feet from under the covers onto the cold parquet floor. I shuffled one foot in front of the other to the bathroom. Under the hissing shower, I drowned out my inner demons with the words drummed into me as a child: *"Our Father who art in Heaven"*.

"God Forgive me. It's all my fault," I cried as the steam fogged my eyes. I blamed myself for what I could have done, what I should have done, what I didn't do, and what I would do, given just one more day with Roger.

His last words on the phone to me were, "I'm tired, Mum." I had answered, "Get some rest, son."

He never answered his phone again. Why didn't I go straight over there, right that minute? I could pray all I wanted, but I couldn't forgive myself.

I grabbed the towel to dry myself under the glare of the bathroom light, avoiding my reflection in the mirror, a ghost of me. I rubbed lotion over my winter-blue-tinged skin from hairline to toes, massaging my arms and legs to ease the adrenalin rush. My fingers dabbed foundation over my pale face, eyes closed to seal the tears inside.

"What time is it?" I asked no one, startling Mr. Kitty, who lay on guard at my feet. Another rush of anxiety pulsed through me as I checked the time.

"Ah, thank God, I can make it."

Today was my second appointment at the hospital with Dr. Bruno. I couldn't be late.

My intake into the Women's Mental Health program as an outpatient didn't change my world with a flick of a switch, but there was a glimmer of hope. I saw it in Dr. Bruno's eyes—unwavering and steady. I heard it in her soothing voice.

"We're a team here."

The hope she gave me reinforced my pillars of faith and friendship. I'd long stopped bleeding my grief onto my friends; I kept it between me and God, and now I had a team.

Dr. Bruno prescribed psychotherapy, and in time my wellness team grew to include Leslie, a social worker. She was tall and blonde, with a bohemian style that made me smile. Her small office reflected her aesthetic, soft around the edges. Colourful cushions cheered the two-seat sofa set against the wall.

"Hello, Irene." Leslie motioned for me to sit down. "I understand the disease of addiction through my experience in the Rapid Access Addiction Medicine Clinic downstairs."

My thoughts wandered. What if Roger had accessed that clinic? Would he be here talking with her instead of me? *What if … what if …*

Leslie's use of words also struck me. Until Roger passed, I had no language around drug use and death and how certain words can add to the stigma. Roger wasn't an addict. He was a young man who suffered from a substance use disorder. Even the word "overdose" carried negative connotations. Roger didn't consume a large dose of drugs that fateful night. It was the toxicity of fentanyl that overcame him.

Leslie pulled me back from the brink of my spiralling thoughts.

"Talk to me. What can I do to help?"

Somewhere between sobs, I grasped that I wasn't alone with my mental collapse. I had held on for so long. The lifeline Leslie offered supported me. I could fall, fall, fall, and before I hit the bottom, she pulled me back to the safety of the couch, reassuring me I would be okay. I had a course of twenty-six therapy sessions with her.

Just as the Humber River swelled and burst its banks with the spring melt, words frozen in my trauma burst into my sessions with Leslie and onto the pages of my notebook.

I was sorry to leave the sanctuary of Lesley's couch, but she assured me I was ready for the next step. I was so proud of the certificate of completion I received. It was an achievement, a baby step towards sanity.

I had frequent check-ins with Dr. Bruno and the team recommended a group program—ACT, Acceptance Commitment Therapy with Andrea, an occupational therapist. I grasped at every opportunity to get well and committed to the program. The regular schedule gave me structure, and I bonded with the other participants as we worked together to set life goals. I felt engaged in the group workshops—mindfulness exercises, writing, art, even games. The daily commute downtown for 9 a.m., three days a week, made me feel almost normal. Andrea encouraged us to set daily routines, even for the weekends, and I found the courage to volunteer at Sistering, a local shelter, a couple of hours on the other two days.

I felt a sense of peace every time I walked through the revolving doors of Women's College Hospital. I knew I was safe here. I was "working" to climb out of the abyss of my PTSD.

Flags of Hope Toronto

June – August 2018

Therapy gave me tools to cope with my grief, but I couldn't ignore the collective grief shared on the Moms Stop the Harm website. Scrolling through the posts, despair hit me. Then I saw the words: "Flags of Hope." The word "Hope" pulled me in. I followed the breadcrumbs of possibility to another site, "Change the Face of Addiction." There, I read about Karen Huggins, a mother in Calgary, Alberta, who had lost her son, Nathan, to opioid poisoning. She had created the Flags of Hope project. I clicked on the link and these words flickered across my screen: "Prayer flags spread the feeling of hope and love in tragic times. It brings those in grief together and honours those they have lost."

The post featured images of a colourful display of over four hundred flags in the atrium of Calgary City Hall. This was in commemoration of International Overdose Awareness Day. Leaning closer to my screen, I read on: "Creating flags to commemorate each life lost to an opioid overdose, and to send them well wishes in the afterlife."

Those flags of hope and love kindled a spark of purpose in my heart. I requested to join the group and sent a message to the host. Karen's daughter, Jessica, replied. I told her I'd like to bring this initiative to Toronto, and we set up a phone call. She told me how the grassroots, community-based Flags of Hope workshops were spreading awareness across Canada.

"How can I get started, Jessica? I'd like to hold a workshop here in Toronto."

She connected me with Christine Dobbs, who had just done a successful workshop in Calgary. Chris was a member of the Moms Stop the Harm group. I read the CBC interview she had posted there, with a picture of her son, Adam, an electrician, who had passed away at twenty-seven.

It read: "Christine Dobbs is on a mission to make sure her son, and others like him, did not die in vain. She wants to give hope to those grieving and provide an opportunity to share their stories with each other and make beautiful flags."

I called Chris. We talked about Adam, and I told her about Roger. We bonded over our shared grief. She was generous with her advice for the flag workshop. I was scribbling notes, but she said, "Don't worry Irene, I'll send you a packet with instructions."

By the time I put the phone down, we were friends. It wasn't long before a big manila envelope arrived in the mail. It included a detailed list of art supplies we would need, plus stencils and a template for cutting and hemming the squares. I couldn't have taken on the project without her.

Moms Stop the Harm had prompted me to ask the Prime Minister to "Do Something." Now I was ready to do something: "Flags of Hope Toronto" was born.

It was June, and we had a couple of months to plan for the big event, International Overdose Awareness Day on August 31. The initiative tied in with my ongoing group therapy of goal-oriented activities and participation in social programs.

First, we had to make the flags! I arranged a workshop at my apartment for August 17. It takes a village, and my Ohana showed up. Lee loaned me her sewing machine and remnants of white fabric. The Christmas elves transformed into summer angels brandishing scissors and irons. It was a hot summer night and my living room resembled a sweatshop. We cut and hemmed over three hundred eight-inch squares—prayer flags to commemorate the three hundred and three opioid deaths reported in Toronto in 2017.

I needed a public space to host the flag-making workshop—a central location close to the TTC for easy access. I thought of a school hall or a library. I contemplated this as I exited the Women's College Hospital following a therapy session. As I walked towards City Hall, I envisioned the flags on display in Nathan Phillips Square. I continued through Trinity Square towards the Eaton Centre and caught sight of the Church of the Holy Trinity. I stopped in my tracks at The Toronto Homeless Memorial outside. It listed names of those who had died because of homelessness in Toronto. I was shaken.

I remembered going into the church once with Roger. He had taken refuge there during his darkest times. The church functioned as a community center for those in need. A sixth sense guided me inside. I knelt at the altar and prayed. The sunlight glinted through the stained-glass window above, reflecting off the organ pipes. It dawned on me that this was the perfect place to hold our event. Maybe there was a basement we could use. I asked a volunteer for directions to the office. There I met Margot, nestled behind a desk, computer humming. She had a kind smile and grey hair framed her small face. Despite being occupied, she greeted me with a smile.

"Hello, I'm Irene," I said. "Do you have a moment?"

"How can I help?"

She invited me to sit down, and I told her about the project and my need for a venue. I pulled out Roger's memorial photo to show her and explained his connection with the church. The church had experience with the opioid crisis and Margot understood the need for awareness and advocacy; their community hub ministered to the most vulnerable in Toronto's downtown core. We went over the details and she checked the calendar for a date near Overdose Awareness Day. Margot offered me the back of the church's main floor for August 30, from 10 a.m. to 1 p.m. She gave me her card and took my email address; we would keep in touch and formalize everything before the day.

"What will you need?"

"I could use six banquet-size tables with chairs. I'll provide all the supplies, table covers, and I'll take care of the cleanup."

She agreed, and we shook hands.

I floated out of the office in disbelief. It was all set.

With the date confirmed, I made a poster to advertise the event. With the support of Moms Stop the Harm, Change the Face of Addiction, and the International Overdose Awareness Day community, the poster spread on social media. To handle the influx of inquiries, I set up a "flagsofhopetoronto" Gmail account. I received requests from those who couldn't attend to make a flag for their loved one. The first flag I decorated was for Adam, Chris's son.

A wave of purpose caught my grief. I was doing something for awareness, while becoming more aware myself.

The next step was buying the art supplies. I had Chris's detailed list:

Acrylic paints in assorted colours

Puff paints

Sponges for stencilling

Paint brushes

Fine point Sharpies

Fabric markers in assorted colours

Plastic tablecloths

Mason jars for water

Twine to string through the flags

One trip to the Dollar Store was all it took. This was a fun task; I felt like a kindergarten teacher preparing for summer camp.

August 30, 2018

It was already sweltering when Lucy and I arrived at the church. I posted flyers at the entrance and around the square to direct people inside. The church staff had set up the banquet tables in the back, away from the altar. Each table had six chairs so we could accommodate thirty-six people at a time. Inside, the church was cool.

I said a wee prayer to myself: *"Dear God, bless us and these flags of hope."*

Before long, Jill, Caro, Rosalie, Jocelyne and others arrived to help set up. We covered the tables and divided out the art supplies, placing a tray of blank flags in the middle of each table. Purple was the colour of overdose awareness, and I had brought dozens of small purple ribbons to pin on them.

It wasn't yet 10 a.m. and I had time to grab a coffee from the cafe. Back in the hall, the girls had taken up their posts and were already painting:

"Someone's Son."

"Someone's Daughter."

"Someone's Dad."

"Someone's Brother."

"Someone's best friend."

We didn't know all their names, but we honoured them in a rainbow of paint and purple hearts.

Jill wrote with the markers, "To the Beautiful Souls who Entered our Lives and Touched our Hearts."

As solemn as it was, there were smiles and camaraderie. We were stronger together.

People wandered in, some to pray, others for a free sandwich and water. Curiosity prompted them to linger, and many shared personal stories of loss. They, too, asked to make flags. Soon the tables were full of participants, transforming the plain white squares with remembrance and condolences. Leana, Roger's old girlfriend, came by. She painted Roger's name surrounded by a lei of Hawaiian flowers and sunbeams. My heart broke for her, for all of us. The church's arched ceilings filled with quiet voices of remembrance. It was a sacred space that reflected the Tibetan tradition of prayer flags, "To commemorate with compassion, the lives lost, and to send them well wishes in the afterlife."

We strung the painted flags of hope on twine to dry outside, fifteen at a time, between the trees lining Trinity Square. They fluttered in the breeze, each one a prayer for somebody's someone. Office workers out for lunch and shoppers heading to the Eaton Centre stopped to admire the colourful flags that resembled festive bunting from a distance. A closer look shocked them, when they realized the display represented the human casualties of the opioid crisis.

The CBC sent a camera crew to cover the event. Standing in the bright sunshine between the trees that held Roger's flags, I shared my story while the flags spoke louder than my words.

By 2 p.m., the flags were dry and it was time to pack up. With Margot's permission, we folded and stored them in boxes under a back bench. We would return tomorrow for the Overdose Awareness Day march. The Holy Trinity Church held the prayers of many. Now it gave our prayer flags sanctuary for the night.

August 31, 2018

International Overdose Awareness Day

"A Time to Remember, A Time to Act"

I woke early with the sunrise, nervous with the anticipation of our planned march to City Hall. I sat on the balcony sipping tea. This ritual had seen me through four seasons of change, from that helpless stormy night after Roger passed to now, advocating to "Change the Face of Addiction." I had registered the event with International Overdose Awareness Day. Their aim was to reduce the stigma of drug-related deaths and acknowledge the grief felt by families and friends, and remember those who died or were permanently injured from drug overdoses.

I held the "Starfish" story that I planned to recite at the rally. I had first heard it at a workshop in Hawaii. The words had stayed with me:

> One day, a man was walking along the beach when he noticed a boy picking up and gently throwing things into the ocean.
>
> Approaching the boy, he asked: "Young man, what are you doing?"
>
> The boy, throwing starfish back into the ocean, replied: "The surf is up and the tide is going out. If I don't throw them back, they'll die."
>
> The man laughed to himself and said, "Do you realize there are miles and miles of beach and hundreds of starfish?" You can't make any difference."
>
> After listening politely, the boy bent down, picked up another starfish and threw it into the surf. Then smiling at the man, he said; "I made a difference to that one."

I thought: *If we could make a difference to just one person out there today...*

It was a clear sunny day, with no thunder on the horizon. I was to meet the girls at 10 a.m. at the church. I donned my "Moms Stop the Harm" t-shirt and headed out. When I arrived, a crowd had gathered outside in Trinity Square. My Ohana was there: Jill, Rosalie, Loreta, Chrisso, Sandra, and others. Volunteers lined up at the back of the church as we distributed the strings of flags. Two by two, they raised them up, ready for the march.

I took my place at the head of the line, holding up Roger's photo. Two police officers on bikes provided an escort as we marched to Nathan Phillips Square. They stopped the busy traffic on Bay Street to let us pass. This wasn't Roger's first police escort, but it was a positive one. I felt him smiling down at us. In the square, we formed a large circle. Members of Moms Stop the Harm gave speeches, and at noon, as the bells tolled at Old City Hall, we held a minute of silence followed by the remembrance prayer.

Caro and Brandon joined us on their lunch break. Brandon was back and had come to support me and honour his brother. We weren't done yet. Caro suggested we hang the Flags of Hope across the iconic TORONTO sign. Tourists, locals, and an unsuspecting wedding party became part of the rally. The police officers stayed close by, even stopping for photo ops. Eventually, City Hall security came out and asked us to remove the hundreds of flags. Our police escort looked on kindly as we folded them into my buggy. It was late afternoon by the time Jill and I returned to her apartment. We ate and reflected on the day. It was bigger than anything I could have imagined since my initial talk with Chris. Hope, that thing with feathers, took flight.

We had a couple of hours' rest before our next call to action. My request to have the CN Tower illuminated in purple for International Overdose Awareness Day had been approved. Before sunset, Jill and I went to the park beneath the tower. We unfurled the flags and strung them across the trees, conveniently lining the walkway. They fluttered in the warm evening breeze, as crowds milled by on their way to the Ed Sheeren concert at the SkyDome next door. It was now rebranded as the Roger's Centre—I looked over and saw Roger's name lit up in red letters ten-feet tall. I smiled. Roger the Famous would like that.

Strangers stopped to ask us questions about the flags. Many shared their own stories of loved ones lost to the opioid crisis. As the sun set, the iconic tower pulsed with purple light from the ground, up fifteen-hundred feet, to circle the observation deck.

A beacon of hope shone across the flags, the city, and the lake beyond.

Climbing the Wall

June 13, 2019

I heard the rain before I saw it—an ominous drumbeat on the trees outside my window. I pulled the white duvet up to my chin. If I didn't open my eyes, perhaps I could suspend this day. But no, June 13 didn't stop for Roger when he took his last breath. It wouldn't stop for me as I faced this second anniversary.

"Just breathe," I told myself as I tried to practice the mindfulness stress reduction I had learned in therapy.

"Mum, would you like a cup of tea?" Brandon's voice floated in from the kitchen as he rustled up his breakfast. His voice activated the mum-switch in my brain.

"Yes, Brandon, I'll be right out."

I peeled my eyes open. Damp air seeped in through the window and clouds invaded my space. I plodded out of bed in time to see Brandon off to work.

"Are you okay, Mum?"

"Don't worry about me. How are you? I'll see you later." I hugged him goodbye. "I love you."

"Bye, Mum," he waved as he went off to work.

I went back to bed and wallowed, with a hot tea and a heavy heart.

Ping! My phone reminded me that I wasn't alone. Lesley sent a picture of Roger's rosebush from her garden in Scotland.

> "Coco guarding Roger's Roses. Buds just coming out. Sending
> you big hugs and so much love, Lesley."

Ping! Lorraine, Roger's godmother, sent me an update on the memorial pear tree she had planted in Portugal.

"No fruit yet … I know every day is hard, but this is the anniversary of the darkest day of your life. I feel for you so much. Oh, if only your dear boy hadn't got on that bloody tram that evening. I think of that so many times. Big hug. I hope you can go somewhere and spend some time with another of your lovely friends. Please don't spend the day alone. Love you, Lorraine xxx."

The night before, Lee and I had gone to Sushi Maido for dinner in Roger's memory, reliving the last supper I had shared with him there. Afterwards, we drove to the parking lot at Queen and Jarvis. We lit candles in mason jars and spread white rose petals, along with tears, on the cold cracked concrete, just as we'd done on Roger's first anniversary.

"Roger, I'll never forget you and this sacred spot," I prayed.

Ping! Ping! Ping! More condolences flooded in. I pushed myself to get up and make breakfast, hot oatmeal with fresh berries. I turned the stove on under the milky mixture and walked away, disoriented with thoughts of Roger. The smoke detector snapped me back to reality as acrid smoke filled the kitchen. I grabbed the blackened pot and ran it out to the patio.

"To hell with breakfast!" I cried.

I turned on music to find solace in the soundtrack from Roger's memorial. Ukuleles filled the air and took me back to happier days of his childhood on the sun-soaked Big Island of Hawaii. I lit a tea light and placed it in the arms of the angel statue that stood guard over his bronze urn. He smiled at me from the memorial picture.

"Aww Roger, what happened?"

I made a cup of coffee and sat by the living room window, not trusting my legs to hold me up. The rain continued to drum in harmony with my tears. Then, the song "Remember Me" from the movie Coco came on and the lyrics floated across the room on a jaunty Mexican tune.

What the heck? This wasn't on Roger's soundtrack … but it was now. I smiled through my tears. "Roger, is that you up to your old tricks again?"

Soon after he passed, I had a dream about Roger. He was dressed in a long white robe and stroked a long beard like a sage. He smiled and said, *"Don't worry, I'm okay, Mum."*

"Where are you?"

"I can't tell you where I am. I'm in the witness protection program."

I reached for him, and he dissolved into white orbs of light.

Roger had a good sense of humour when he was alive, and it permeated the void between us now.

I let the day drain away with my tears. We had a plan, but I wasn't feeling up for it. Roger's friends Shay and Justin had arranged a night at the Basecamp Climbing Gym with Brandon. Leana was joining us. This would be our second annual "Climb to the Top for Roger". Climbing was Brandon's passion. Most nights, you could find him at the gym. How could I miss that? It was 5 p.m. and I was still in my pyjamas. Oh God, I had to be there at 6 p.m. I dragged myself into the shower, face swollen and tear stained. I couldn't let them down. I couldn't let Roger down.

Then I received a text from Brandon: "Mom, bring me Roger's Raptor's jacket to wear later."

My heart jumped. Brandon had barely mentioned his brother's name since he passed. It was too hard for him. Now, here he was asking for Roger's prized jacket. It was a black silk bomber jacket with black and red ribbing and "TORONTO" in red letters across the front. Taking it out of the closet, I could smell the mix of Roger's tobacco and musky cologne. I buried my head in it, inhaling my son's aroma. It melted my heart to think Brandon would wear it to cheer on the Raptors. He was opening up. The gulf between us all was closing.

Last year at Basecamp, I had joined the boys to cheer them on and take pictures. Tonight was different; for the first time, I would climb, too. Brandon smiled as he introduced me to the staff to get fitted up with the gear.

"Way to go, Mum."

I laughed and asked if they had a senior-citizen's discount.

Walking onto the padded gym floor, excitement echoed up to the ceiling. The gym smelled of sweat and pulsed with physical exertion. I strained my neck to watch bodies scaling the walls like monkeys. Was I mad? What was on that waiver I had signed?

Roger's friends watched as Brandon tied the belay rope in an intricate figure-eight knot to my harness. I was learning the lingo now. My first attempt at the sheer vertical wall with the colour-coded grips was cautious. It was a beginner's route, and I made it three-quarters of the way up. They all clapped and cheered like I had scaled the Matterhorn. I was dizzy and came down and took a break. I watched them take turns on the more intricate manoeuvres. Shay and Leana had worked their way through a few levels. Brandon was an encouraging coach. He pointed out the finer elements of using the right muscle groups and breathing.

"Do you want another turn, Mum?" he asked.

"Why not!"

This time, I went for a higher level; the grips looked close enough together. I tied up again and Brandon said, "You can do it, Mum. Use your legs."

He took the rope to guide me. I made it a third of the way up, then I felt my arms and legs shake like Jell-O. I looked down and motioned to him to release me. They all cheered.

"Go Mum, go Mum!"

I looked up at that bloody wall and said, "Roger, I'm climbing for you!"

With all my might, I pushed on my legs and flung one arm over the other to grab the next grip up, then the next foot, and then another grip.

I heard Brandon say, "I got you, Mum," and felt the rope tighten as I propelled my body to the top. A cheer went up. I did it! My boy had my back as he held the line. Brandon relaxed the rope, and I floated down to the floor.

"Come on, the game's starting," Brandon reminded us.

"Let's go to the Pour Boy. Last night, I saw them carry in a flat-screen TV."

He put on Roger's jacket and we followed him as he swaggered across the street. I'd never seen him so confident.

We went upstairs to the funky fusion bar in Korea town, no bigger than my living room. The huge flat-screen TV beamed the game across the room. The Raptors were already ahead by a couple of points. This was the NBA Championship, and

Toronto could win. The Raptors' score was up, down, then up. I had whiplash following the team as they darted, dribbled, and dunked up and down the court. By the last minute, we were all screaming,

"Go Raptors! Go Raptors!"

In the heat of the fervour, Brandon had thrown off Roger's jacket. I grabbed it and put it on.

"Come on Roger, put in a word for your team," I yelled.

In the final second, Kyle Lowry nailed the winning shot. I turned and saw my usually placid Brandon standing on the chair, fist pumping and cheering at the top of his lungs. The entire room exploded.

We won!

A day that had dawned with dread had turned into a celebration.

Surfer Silhouette

November 2019

Golden maple leaves swirled around the emptied swimming pool outside as I stood sandwiched at the kitchen island between the oven and the overflowing living room. I marvelled at Landy as she ducked and weaved from the cupboard to the stove.

"Nope, not quite ready," she announced as the oven door slammed shut, but not before a face full of steam escaped to herald the turkey roasting inside. Landy stopped for a moment and we all inhaled the aroma of roasting juices. Then she clicked back into gear. Drinks were poured and appetizers were passed around.

The Anderson family, a jubilant, boisterous clan, gathered for a Thanksgiving feast. This was Roger's Ohana—his family. Landy practically adopted him when her daughter, Leana, brought him home to visit several years earlier. Roger had eyed the pot of sticky rice steaming on the stove and beamed, "I love sticky rice!" He stole Landy's heart with his appetite for Chinese food and his easy smile. He loved Leana and fit into her family. Her Metis, Chinese, and Scottish heritage aligned with his Chinese and Scottish roots. It was a match made in Heaven.

Now he was in Heaven, and I stood at the kitchen island in his place. The Andersons were a tight-knit family and I was honoured to be their guest. Everyone was in motion—generations of family and extended family weaved and bobbed around, music played loud, and our voices were louder so we could be heard over the din.

Leana and her sister Jordan squeezed on either side of me like a big hug. We chatted and their faces lit up.

"We're going to Hawaii," Leana said. Her voice floated towards me. The words seemed suspended in the hot kitchen air.

"Hawaii!" I leaned in, pressing my hands to the counter to stop them from shaking.

"Yes, we'll be staying in Oahu and then we want go to the Big Island for a few days to see where Roger grew up."

Roger and Leana had dreamed of going to the Big Island together one day.

"We could take Roger's ashes and lay them in the ocean," Leana said—she had a small urn from Roger's memorial.

The weight in her words, coupled with the sadness that swept over her face, broke open my heart. The noise and bustle of the kitchen evaporated from my ears.

"Are any of Roger's friends on the island?" she asked.

"Let me think. Who could show you around? It's a big island," I said.

Every fibre of my being knew I should accompany these precious girls and escort my boy home. I could show them our old house overlooking the Kohala coast, his old school, and the places he played and worked. I knew the exact beach to lay his ashes. This was a trip I'd taken in my mind many times since Roger passed. I hadn't had the strength to make it yet. A cold sweat trickled down my back.

"The turkey is ready," Landy's voice brought me back. Our conversation was shelved as dinner was served, complete with sticky rice.

"Aww Roger, you should be here," I thought. I felt the joy he had expressed to me whenever he spoke about Leana's family.

Later that evening, Leana drove me to the GO Train station in Oshawa. My heart was as heavy as the rainfall. We hugged goodbye.

"Thanks for coming," Leana said. Her long, black hair reflected the pool of light from the overhead parking lot lamps.

"I'll email you tomorrow with all the info on the Big Island," I reassured her. "Send me your dates. I'll get someone to show you around."

Our voices were drowned out as the double-decker train screeched into the station. I walked towards the hulking machine emblazoned with tall green letters, "GO".

"GO," I repeated as I climbed on board, choosing to sit upstairs in the almost vacant carriage. I leaned my forehead against the cold window, the platform below puddled in the misty light.

"I have to GO," I mouthed the words to no one.

"But you can't afford it," replied the wee voice in my head.

"To hell with poverty," I argued with myself.

"What should I do, Roger?" I prayed.

My resolve strengthened as the train gathered speed. *"GO, GO, GO!"* the grinding wheels screeched at me. I felt a push, or was it a shove, as the train ground to a halt at the next station, I fell back in my seat.

"Call Jen," I thought—or was that Roger speaking to me?

I reached into my bag for my phone and pressed the icon of Jen's smiling face, fringed with blonde hair. The phone rang across the miles.

"Hi Irene, what's up?" I heard Jen's sweet Minnesotan drawl.

"Jen, I just left Landy's. The girls are going to Hawaii," I stuttered as the train revved up again. "I need to go with them. It's time to take Roger home."

"Yes," she said, like she was expecting my call. "I'll come with you."

Of course she would. To Hell with poverty indeed. If ever there was a need to use my line of credit, it was now. And so it was that three weeks later, Jen and I greeted Leana and Jordan with a refrain of "Aloha" as they arrived at Kona Airport on the Big Island. We adorned them with leis. Leana plucked a plumeria and placed it behind her ear with a big smile. Her beauty rivalled any of the island girls. We fell into a group hug as the dazzling sunlight dappled through the palm trees. We linked arms and walked to the waiting car.

The next day, the soles of our feet felt the golden sand of Mauna Lani beach while the rhythm of soft waves kissed our toes. Roger's feet first touched this beach in 1990 when he was barely two years old. He toddled, splashed, and grew to swim with the turtles on this Hawaiian shore. He learned to boogie board and catch waves. He was a free-spirited child, fearless of jumping into the deep end. It was here at Mauna Lani resort that he attended preschool and kindergarten.

His dad, Henry, and I worked at the luxury Orchid at Mauna Lani resort hotel. This was the same beach where I went into labour with Brandon during the annual turtle release. Roger's pre-school class had accompanied the procession of young honu (turtles) squirming to free themselves into the warm Pacific Ocean. The honu is the Hawaiian symbol of good luck, a guardian spirit. It was divine providence that my boy's spirit should find release in these waters.

As a teenager, Roger's fearless nature fed on the adrenalin rush of edgy sports, like skateboarding and surfing. He was more apt to drive his truck to the beach than to Kealakehe High School, especially when the surf was up. He dropped out of school in his final year. This had prompted my decision to return to Toronto in 2007 with the boys in the hope of a better future. Roger didn't embrace the move at first but followed eventually in 2010. By his twenties, the illness of addiction had caged his spirit. He fought fiercely to overcome the demons. It was during one two-year recovery period that he met Leana as she walked her Cane Corso dog past the recovery home in Oshawa.

Roger, sitting on the porch steps, had called out, "That's some dog you have there."

Leana had smiled and brought Jax over for Roger to admire.

"He reminds me of the Hawaiian hunting dogs," Roger had continued, and they chatted and walked together to the corner. The noble broker Jax brought them together. Before long, Roger was walking Leana home into the kitchen. That's Leana's story to tell, but I saw the love in his eyes at the mere mention of her name. Even with my love, her love, and the support of all our Ohana, it wasn't enough.

We four broken-hearted women embraced our memories of Roger. I held his ashes close to my heart in a small bronze urn. Jen set the flowers we'd picked that morning from the lush slopes of Pololu Valley into the kayak. The scent of plumeria and tuberose wafted on the warm ocean breeze. Jen and I waded into the turquoise water and pushed the kayak off the beach. The girls paddled behind us. The sun shone above the snow-capped summit of Mauna Kea and bowed behind a wisp of a cloud. Palm trees saluted our regatta.

When we reached the calm waters beyond the reef break, Leana and Jordan pulled their paddleboards alongside our kayak. We held a moment of silence. Roger's life reeled in technicolour through the cinema of my mind.

"It's time," I said, gulping back my tears as I twisted the lid off the small vase.

I looked over the kayak into the fathomless ocean, and wondered if the honu were waiting in the depths to escort my boy home.

A hand took the urn and shook his ashes into the blue. Was it mine? I was out of my body, floating above the scene. We scattered a rainbow of Hawaiian flowers across the ocean surface. At that moment, a swell barrelled across the bay. Our kayak rose high and bobbed as the wave peeled towards Hapuna Beach. The kind of wave surfers dream of. I felt Roger's spirit catch it.

I exhaled and recited an ode I had written the night before, inspired by a poem by Elizabeth Fry. The words had taken shape as I sat on the lanai under the pitch-black Kohala sky, perforated with a million stars:

> Do not weep.
>
> I do not sleep.
>
> I am the ocean breeze that blows across the surf at Mauna Lani where the honu play.
>
> I am the diamond glint of moonlight on snow-capped Mauna Kea.
>
> I am the sun on ripened papayas.
>
> I am the mist rising from Akaka Falls
>
> When you awaken in the morning's hush.
>
> I am in the swift uplifting rush of the Pueo in circled flight.
>
> I am the Northern star that shines in the Kohala sky at night.
>
> Do not cry.
>
> I am here with you always.

Roger caught the wave on Mauna Lani Bay, hanging ten in the big surf of Heaven.

About the Author

Irene Reilly is a Scottish Canadian writer, mother, and advocate. Born in Glasgow, she immigrated to Canada, raised her two sons in Hawaii while working in the hospitality industry, and now calls Toronto home. She is a graduate of the University of Toronto's School of Continuing Studies Creative Writing Program, and a facilitator for the Writers Collective of Canada.

Irene lost her son to fentanyl poisoning and became a powerful advocate in building awareness of Canada's opioid crisis with her Flags of Hope Toronto initiative. She has partnered with Moms Stop the Harm, Families for Addiction Recovery, Black CAP, and International Overdose Awareness Day to raise awareness and end the stigma associated with substance-use harms and related toxicity.

Her first memoir, *OHANA: Love, Grief and Hope in the Time of the Opioid Crisis*, is her story of love, loss, and resilience dedicated to the memory of her son Roger and all those struggling with or lost to the crisis.

Acknowledgements

Thank you, **John Collins,** for your painting, "Surfer Silhouette ll", and for permission to use it as the cover of this book. Fate brought us together at Huggo's when we came for lunch after Roger's memorial in Hawaii. John's work can be found at Kona Seaside Gallery: www.konaseasidegallery.com/

I am grateful for the **University of Toronto** and its School of Continuing Studies, Creative Writing Program. I thank each of my instructors throughout the course. I workshopped many of the scenes in this book in your classes. I am indebted to **Marina Nemet** for your guidance throughout my final project, a collection of short stories which form the backbone of this book. On the first day of our first Introduction to Writing class in 2015, I met **Joan** who became my friend and writing partner. I couldn't have completed this book without you.

Writers Collective of Canada (WCC) has been a source of inspiration since my first workshop. Thank you to Jesse Cohoon for your inspiration and introduction to the WCC, then known as the Toronto Writers Collective. Thank you to Siobhan Lant who mentored me as I trained to become a writing facilitaor in the program. My gratitude goes out to my co-facilitator and friend Nadja. *"When we write with others we discover ourselves."*

Angie Hamilton, your friendship and collaboration are the cornerstones of my advocacy. Thank you for everything you do for so many, through **Families for Addiction Recovery (FAR).**

Moms Stop the Harm—including Petra Schultz, Lesley McBain, and the whole team at MSTH—have given me community and connection through advocacy. Thank you.

John Ryan and your team at **International Overdose Awareness Day (IOAD),** I am indebted to you for the support and tools I used to launch the Flags of Hope Overdose Awareness Day effort in Toronto in 2018. 2024 marked our eighth annual Overdose Awareness Day at City Hall.

Kevin, Mike, and Heather at Renascent: Roger's road to recovery began with you. Thank you for giving me back my boy; we treasure the years we had prior to his fatal relapse. Heather, my road to understanding the disease of addiction began with you—thank you for the family program. Caro, you captured Roger's recovery in your interview with us for the Renascent annual report in 2014. You also captured our hearts. Your friendship lit up Roger's life and stays with me today.

Jordan Anderson and all the team at Alpha House: the home environment and counselling your community provided Roger during his recovery journey gave him confidence, happiness, and everlasting friendships.

Earlier versions of some chapters in this book were first platformed by these editors and publications. I am grateful to them:

"A Tale of Two Tables" twice by Alanna Rusnak publishing, first in December 2019 in *Blank Spaces* magazine, then in the *Just Words* anthology in 2020.

"The End of My World" in the Writers Collective of Canada *Front Lines: Until the Words Run Pure* anthology from its *Write On!* Program in 2020. Thank you to Jesse Cohoon, Editor, and Susan Ksiezopolski, my *Write On!* mentor.

"Carpet Diem" in *Voices 2020*, a Toronto Writers Cooperative anthology. Thank you to John Miller, Editor, and his team.

"Surfer Silhouette" in the Writers Collective of Canada *Front Lines: Courage, Without a Parachute* anthology from its *Write On!* Program in 2022. Thank you to Jesse Cohoon, Editor, and Anna Lee-Popham, my *Write On!* mentor that year.

The Starfish Story on page 103 is adapted from Loren Eiseley's essay "The Star Thrower", published in *The Unexpected Universe* (1969) by Harcourt, Brace and World. In the same chapter, the phrase "Hope, that thing with feathers", is a reference to Emily Dickinson's poem titled "'Hope' is the thing with feathers".

The opening poem, "Woven" by Becky Hemsley, is from the 2023 book *When I Am Gone* and is used here with permission of its author.

Resources

Alpha House

www.alphahousetoronto.ca

Families for Addiction Recovery

www.farcanada.org

Moms Stop the Harm

www.momsstoptheharm.com

Renascent

www.renascent.ca

Writers Collective of Canada

www.wcc-cec.org

International Overdose Awareness Day
31 August

TORONTO

www.ingramcontent.com/pod-product-compliance
Lightning Source LLC
Chambersburg PA
CBHW070333090426
42733CB00012B/2460